Curing the Gilded Cage

Susanna Mittermaier

Curing the Gilded Cage
Copyright © 2025 Susanna Mittermaier
Access Consciousness Publishing
ISBN: 978-1-63493-706-1 (paperback)
ISBN: 978-1-63493-707-8 (ebook)
Access Consciousness Publishing
www.acpublishing.com

All rights reserved. No part of this publication may be reproduced, stored in a retrieval system, or transmitted, in any form or by any means electronic, mechanical, photocopying, recording, or otherwise without prior written permission from the publisher.

The author and publisher of the book do not make any claim or guarantee for any physical, mental, emotional, spiritual, or financial result. All products, services and information provided by the author are for general education and entertainment purposes only. The information provided herein is in no way a substitute for medical or other professional advice. In the event you use any of the information contained in this book for yourself, the author and publisher assume no responsibility for your actions.

Contents

Chapter 1 - How Much of Your Life Is Really Yours? 6

Chapter 2 - The Start of Change: Being Present 9
    The Being Present Exercise 11

Chapter 3 - Rightness the Ultimate Cage 15
    Presumptive Realities 17

Chapter 4 - What Do You Need? 23
    Reactive Realities 26

Chapter 5 - Relationships… From Cage to Creation 31

Chapter 6 - Let the Games Begin 42

Chapter 7 - Choice… the Beginning of New Adventures .. 45

Chapter 8 - When Your Body Is No Longer Your Cage 49

Chapter 9 - Pain 53
Being a Healer 57

Chapter 10 - Psychological Cages 60
Caring 62
Stress 63

Chapter 11 - The Ease Consciousness Can Bring 67
Gaslighting 69

Chapter 12 - What Is Next in Your Life? 77

Chapter 13 - What Does It Take To Cure the Gilded Cage? 84
Turn on the Lights 84
Do You Need to Be Right? 85
Choice Creates 85
What Do You Know? 85
Relax 86
Being Different – Being You 86
Courage 87
Vulnerability 88
Ease 89
Joy 90
Glory 91

Chapter 14 - The Unsuccessful Savior 95

Chapter 15 - Beyond Labels 101
Can Feelings and Emotions Be Labels? 102

Chapter 16 - Question Everything! 108

Chapter 17 - Being Crazy and Mental Illness 111
   Does the World Make Sense to You? 113
   Have You Ever Tried to Heal Insanity? 115
   People Choose Their Insanity. 115

Chapter 18 - Do You Still Need Your Story? 118
   Family 120
   Kindness for You 123
   Dramatic or Pragmatic? 124

Chapter 19 - Beyond the Cage! Your Future Is Calling. ... 126
   How Big Is Your Ask? 126
   Explore Your Ask! 127

What is Pragmatic Psychology? 135

The Access Consciousness Clearing Statement® 137
   A Pragmatic Tool Hidden in Plain Sight 137
   Every Problem is a Possibility in Disguise 138
   How Do You See Your Life? 138

Susanna Mittermaier 142

Chapter 1

How Much of Your Life Is Really Yours?

At the age of 27, amidst the excitement of beginning my career as a psychologist and settling into our first home with my boyfriend, a nagging sense of unease lingered beneath the surface.

Despite the outward appearance of a perfect life, I couldn't shake the feeling that something crucial was missing. It was as though I was living a life that belonged to someone else – fulfilling the expectations of others while neglecting my own needs and desires.

The turning point came when the weight of this realization became unbearable, manifesting in waves of depression and frustration.

I began to understand that my emotional turmoil was a direct result of the choices I had made and the life I had constructed. So, was I going to continue down this path of misery or summon the courage to forge a new one? Was I going to allow myself to sink further into depression or was I going to swim towards a different reality?

When I chose to break free from the confines of societal expectations, it was uncomfortable and one of the toughest experiences in my life.

It meant risking the disappointment and disapproval of those who had come to expect a certain version of me. It was like sending out wedding invitations and then realizing that the ceremony was not a celebration of love but rather a performance for others' expectations, other people's happiness at the cost of my own.

Yet, in that moment of reckoning, I made the choice to reclaim my life—to prioritize my own happiness over the comfort of conformity. Once I stood strong in my decision, it marked the rebirth of my true self.

By choosing what is true for me, everything shifted. Relationships were tested, boundaries were redrawn, but through it all, I emerged stronger and more resilient.

In retrospect, I realize that many people like me are unwittingly trapped in lives that do not belong to them. Some wait until the pain becomes unbearable before they dare to break free. Others continue to believe they don't have a choice.

But what if there is another choice? What if we could choose freedom without hitting rock bottom?

My journey taught me that we have the power to design our lives according to our own terms—to prioritize our own happiness and fulfillment. It's not always easy, and there will be challenges along the way, but the freedom that comes from being who we truly are is worth every moment of discomfort.

To anyone who finds themselves in a similar predicament, I urge you to listen to the whispers of your being. Embrace your truth, even if it means upsetting those around you. For in the end, the only approval that truly matters, is your own.

CHAPTER 2

The Start of Change: Being Present

To ignite change, learn to embrace being present in your life, by truly seeing and being aware of everything around you. We are often only fully present in emergencies, when life demands it. Otherwise, it is our phones and endless thoughts that distract us from experiencing the richness of now.

Observe people outside: how many are truly present, and how many operate on autopilot? How often do we search for something right in front of us? Being present means not missing a thing and that offers a distinct advantage. Are you overwhelmed by being present or by the energy spent erecting barriers against experiencing life?

Being present requires practice; for the longest time we have been conditioned to check out as a coping mechanism. What we fail to realize is, that this limits us from receiving what we desire. In a world valuing entertainment, we've relinquished our ability to create, we have let external sources dictate our focus. In today's reality, children who were once curious and inventive, now often prioritize screens over play.

By being present, we reclaim power over our lives. We can start by asking, "What is fun for me? What brings me joy?" This question marks the beginning of redefining your life. It starts with embracing the present, acknowledging your choices and asking questions that unveil the essence of the life you genuinely aspire to craft.

For instance, you can start the day by not turning to your phone as soon as we wake up and instead spend time with yourself, becoming clear on what you would like, your wishes and what is true for you.

Being present transforms your outlook, turning life into a thrilling adventure. Have you envisioned what constant presence might entail? What if it's different from your expectations? Imagine the abundance awaiting when you fully embrace life. How much more accessible would possibilities become, easing your journey? And yes, consider the financial gains such as money – the magic word, "money," has your attention. Intrigued?

Let's dive in and explore together!

The Being Present Exercise

Harnessing your body is key to being present. It naturally resides in the now. Place your hands on your body, feeling the earth beneath your feet or the support of your chair. Just three points of connection - hands, body and feet - can re-ignite being present. Acknowledge your body; it's easy to forget its existence.

Yet, realize you're not confined to it; you extend beyond, into boundless space. Expand your awareness outward, encompassing the room, city, continent, and beyond, while remaining attuned to your physical form.

Navigating this skill may take practice, especially amid others' limited perspectives. But you don't have to conform; you hold the power to choose expansiveness. Being present allows quick recognition of unwanted paths, giving you the endless ability to steer your own course.

Whose vibration are you wearing?

Consider your typical demeanor: are you typically cheerful or more subdued, content with normalcy or brimming with happiness? Have you ever paused to question whose energy you're embodying?

Now, envision yourself in nature—a place of your choosing, be it by the ocean, amidst mountains, or within the tranquil woods—for three weeks or longer. How would you be? Many individuals lack insight into their true beings, assuming their image defines them without question.

How frequently do you unknowingly absorb the frequencies of others, like wearing someone else's clothes without realizing it? Just as communities often unite around shared energies, whether among friends, cultures, or families. I have worked with many individuals who are often surprised to realize that they are happier, freer and experience more peace than they thought they could. However, as they embrace transformation and flourish, they may encounter resistance from those whose vibrations no longer resonate.

As you grow, you inspire others to do the same, even if they're hesitant because it challenges their choices. But what if your personal growth reflects your own truth and what is true for you, sparking fresh ideas and progress?

Whose energy are you resonating with? Whose requirements are you meeting? What alternatives are available to you? If you prioritized yourself, what energy could you embody?

Choosing to conform, for acceptance might seem appealing. Society often says fitting in means being popular and having friends. But think about it: are those who don't accept your uniqueness really your friends? In many social groups and cultures, there's pressure to be the same.

Even in new places, people often feel this pressure, fearing judgment. But judgments are like farts - trivial. Just as you'd ignore a fart, ignoring judgments saves energy and creativity. Is it worth worrying about?

As owners of a majestic castle in a quaint Italian village, my partners and I faced significant resistance from the locals when we began its renovation. In a community where change is rare and roles are firmly established, new ventures are often met with skepticism. While their attitude was understandable, we chose to persist because we recognized the uniqueness of our vision: a haven of elegance, where history enriches the future.

Through restoration and the incorporation of exquisite antique furnishings, the castle now stands as a boutique hotel and restaurant, offering solace and inspiration to all who visit. Many guests leave transformed, inspired to infuse elegance into their own lives. We think elegance isn't just about how you look but also how you think—a readiness to enjoy plenty with little effort for big outcomes.

When we pursued our vision, the townspeople began to support us. They recognized the uniqueness of our endeavor and actively participated by not only reopening the castle to visitors after decades of closure and providing employment, but also by restoring the entire town to its former beauty.

What began as a divide transformed into unity and collaboration simply because we refused to validate judgments and remained committed to realizing our vision for the future.

What do you see the future can be? What would you have to be willing to be and choose to make that happen? Conforming to uniformity unwittingly entraps many individuals in a cage they fail to recognize.

CHAPTER 3

Rightness the Ultimate Cage

Where do you think you know everything in your life? Once you think you know everything, you stop asking questions. You stop trying new things and just stick to how things are. Even if you want more, you won't find it if you care more about being right than being free. What rightness are you holding onto that, if you let go, would set you free?

The allure of a monarch's life, both in ancient times and today, captivates many with its opulence: the wealth, fame, and status. It's perceived as the pinnacle of success, the epitome of perfection. However, the price of such prestige is steep. Monarchs are bound by rigid expectations, afforded little freedom to shape their own destinies. They are also compelled to maintain a separation from ordinary citizens, further reinforcing their confinement.

Yet, any gilded cage, whether adorned with gold or celebrity, is still a cage. Its splendor may initially blind one to their entrapment, convincing them that they've attained the height of achievement. But as time passes, the glitter fades, leaving behind a sense of emptiness and disillusionment. This phenomenon isn't limited to monarchs; actors and singers, too, fall prey to the trappings of fame, losing sight of their true purpose and succumbing to destructive habits.

Have you ever envisioned standing among the elite, fully embracing the power and prestige that comes with it? If so, are you prepared to rise to the challenge and face the true price of greatness?

Is it only the famous who reside in gilded cages or does the illusion extend further? It's easy to identify the constraints that ensnare others, but have you illuminated the shadows in your own life? Where do you find yourself confined, unaware of the gilded cage that surrounds you?

Presumptive Realities

To break free from the gilded cage, we need to look closely at what keeps us trapped. One thing is assuming things are a specific way. When we assume, we lose control and get stuck in our own views, losing our freedom.

Have you ever felt a burning desire for change, sensing the possibility of something greater, yet feeling powerless to attain it? This is where presumptions trap us, like strict rules limiting our possibilities.

Presumptive realities are assumptions we accept as true without questioning, often shaped by culture or experience. They influence how we see the world and can limit our thinking by making us accept situations as inevitable. By recognizing and challenging these beliefs, we open ourselves to new possibilities.

They dictate our paths, delineating what's feasible and what's not, what's right and what's wrong, leaving us bereft of choice and unable to reshape our lives congruent with our true desires.

But here's the good news: these presumptive realities don't happen to us; we unwittingly allow them to govern our lives. By cultivating presence in our lives, we become adept at recognizing their influence.

How do these presumptive realities wield such power? Through our unwavering belief in them, our blind adherence, and our reluctance to question what else might be possible for us. They mold our reality in ways more invasive than we realize. Anytime we feel burdened or stuck, it's a sign that a presumptive reality is pulling the strings.

Consider a woman I once worked with. Struggling financially and feeling drained by societal expectations, she longed for ease and joy in her life and business. However, she found herself stifled by presumptive realities—believing she had no choice but to meet others' needs and be what they expected of her. These beliefs not only hindered her joy but also obstructed her financial flow.

Once she confronted and challenged these presumptions, she experienced a profound shift. Embracing others' needs of her being someone to look up to and her role as a "star" at an upcoming event, she allowed herself to shine, resulting in unprecedented success—a million euros in a single day. Her transformation illustrates the power of making new choices.

But beware: adopting a new presumptive reality as a solution—such as believing that being a "star" guarantees financial success—only leads to another form of entrapment. True freedom isn't just about our actions; it's about breaking down the beliefs and assumptions that hold us back from what we truly desire. How many presumptive realities are you currently being controlled by that give you no freedom of choice?

Notice what that question is bringing up. No need to think about it. Just get the sense of it. Allow it to apply to you in the way it does. To change anything what is required is choice. That is the main ingredient in changing your life. Let's ask the question again and you can ask yourself what you would like to choose with regards to it.

How many presumptive realities are you currently being controlled by that give you no freedom of choice? What would you like to choose? Will you let go of everything that is keeping this limitation in your world? If it is a "yes" for you, let's use a unique and pragmatic tool to have it be gone from your world. Are you ready?

This can only work if you choose to let it go. It is not something that someone does to you or that just happens. If you make the choice to let it go, let's go for it!

> *Everything that is, times a godzillion, and everything holding all that in place, will you destroy and uncreate it all, please? Yes? Right and wrong, good and bad, POD and POC, all 100, shorts, boys, POVADs, creations, bases and beyonds™.**

*This part above introduces the Access Consciousness clearing statement®, which encourages you to embrace change by releasing, dismantling, and undoing the barriers that uphold limitations. Its effectiveness hinges on your choice and your willingness to allow it to work. Choice is paramount; if you choose to release a limitation, it dissipates.

The clearing statement simply aids in facilitating that choice. It might seem unusual at first. I have personally used this tool in my own life and in numerous sessions, and I've consistently witnessed profound transformations.

If you would like to have an explanation of each part of the clearing statement, you can read more at the back of the book or visit: www.theclearingstatement.com

Are you ready to use it again?

> *How many presumptive realities are you using to limit what you can be choosing? You didn't even think you were choosing your limitations, did you? Everything that is, times a godzillion, will you destroy and uncreate it all? Right and wrong, good and bad, POD and POC, all 100, shorts, boys, POVADs, creations, bases and beyonds.*

You might entertain the thought, "If only I had been aware, I wouldn't have made that choice." Yet, the truth is, you would have. Every decision we make, even if it constrains us, serves a purpose in that moment. It yields the desired outcome, regardless of whether it shows up as a limitation.

Imagine the liberation that comes with acknowledging that the limitations in your life are of your own making. Are there any presumptive realities arising now, suggesting you are wrong for these choices? Keep in mind, there are no inherently right or wrong choices—each one brings valuable awareness and enhances your journey, but only if you are open to it.

What if you embraced every choice, without judgment? How much empowerment would that grant you? Even the choices that seem to confine you - what if you simply owned them, acknowledging, "Yes, I chose those limitations. I acknowledge them, yet I refuse to let them dictate my future. Instead, I accept them as gifts of awareness and forge ahead, stronger than before."

This is where the magic of choice reveals itself.

> *How many presumptive realities are you using to determine what you can never be choosing? Everything that is, times a godzillion, will you destroy and uncreate it all? Right and wrong, good and bad, POD and POC, all 100, shorts, boys, POVADs, creations, bases and beyonds.*

While growing up we were presented with a predetermined menu of choices: "This is what's attainable for you in life, while this isn't." But if you examine each facet of your life - money, body, relationships, career, and more - you will realize these are merely presumptive realities. They function as self-contained spheres, convincing you that you are bound by their limitations, leaving you feeling tethered like a plug into an outlet. You accept these boundaries, believing, "This is the extent of what I can achieve financially, physically, socially, and professionally, and nothing more."

However, this confinement persists only until you recognize the cage for what it truly is. Once you perceive its limitations, they lose their grip on you and you reclaim control over your life.

If you find yourself peering too deeply into the rabbit hole, perhaps it's time to set this book aside or pass it on to someone else - yet if you are brave and are ready to live your life for you, continue reading, for we're just scratching the surface of what's to come!

Chapter 4

What Do You Need?

What do you think you need, that you can choose? Who do you think you need, that you cannot choose?

Are you waiting to be chosen by people? Or are you the one who is choosing?

If you believe you require someone in your life, money, or anything else, you relinquish control of your own destiny. Need only fosters a sense of scarcity.

> *How many presumptive realities do you have inventing need as real? Everything that is, times a godzillion, will you destroy and uncreate it all? Right and wrong, good and bad, POD and POC, all 100, shorts, boys, POVADs, creations, bases and beyonds.*

What could you achieve if you operated from choice rather than necessity? If you selected the individuals in your life based on preference rather than perceived need, what transformations might occur? Imagine if love stemmed from "I choose you" instead of "I need you" - how much richer could your relationships become? Have you ever experienced a breakup, only to realize afterward that you are perfectly content without that person? Embracing this self-sufficiency opens the door to receiving more and taking charge of your life.

Thinking things are a specific way all the time makes you feel needy. It makes you believe you can't change anything and makes everything rigid, like you're stuck on a set path. "I must behave this way because of my upbringing. I must conform because of my gender. I must act a certain way because I'm a parent." But are these beliefs truly your only options? Each time you catch yourself accepting limitations and believing change is impossible, ask, "Is this a presumptive reality?" Recognize it as such, and if you choose to release it, say:

> *Everything that is, I will now destroy and uncreate it, times a godzillion. Right and wrong, good and bad, POD and POC, all 100, shorts, boys, POVADs, creations, bases and beyonds.*

A gilded cage represents the belief that fulfillment comes from external sources and the need to belong to something outside of oneself. It strips away your empowerment, ensnaring you in appearances and attachments that ultimately corrode your well-being.

Whom or what have you convinced yourself you require to attain the life you desire? By relinquishing this sense of need, you pave the way for a life built on your own choices.

Crafting a fulfilling existence isn't a single decision but a series of deliberate choices, each savored without haste. Instead of racing toward the future, what if you embraced each step with the same relaxed enjoyment as a cat, leopard, or giraffe strolling gracefully?

We once welcomed a cat into our home after he appeared at our door one day. He sought affection and food, and initially, we fed him only when we were home. Eventually, we assumed he needed someone to feed him regularly, but did he truly require this? No. He simply utilized his feline charm to manipulate us into caring for him. Recognizing this freed us from unnecessary constraints, allowing us to consider what worked best for both him and us. By transcending presumptive realities, we unlocked new choices.

Reactive Realities

Here emerges another cornerstone of our intricate cages: the tendency to react to circumstances. How much of your precious time is consumed by reactive responses? How frequently do you allow genuine peace, and how long do you permit it to endure? Have you ever found yourself in a situation that others deemed challenging or dramatic, yet you remained serene or found it less daunting than anticipated?

This is when you are being you, acting and creating instead of succumbing to the impulse to react. How long did you allow this ease to persist?

I once worked with a patient who faced the end of her marriage. Despite finding peace with the situation, those around her continually projected their own drama onto her, expecting her to be in turmoil. At times, she compromised her own truth to conform to their expectations, subsequently experiencing periods of sadness. She internalized judgments about her perceived abnormality for not reacting as expected—sad and despondent for an extended period.

We talked about her facing the truth and picking pragmatic possibilities over drama. Being pragmatic means choosing what's true for you and what creates a greater life and future for you without worrying if you are getting it right. When she started doing this, she found it easier to stay happy, even when others expected her to react differently.

Reactive realities are responses to life's challenges that we choose, based on the belief that reacting is what normalcy entails. However, handling tough situations with ease without overreacting questions this view, causing some to feel they must react artificially.

> *How many needs of reactive realities are you using to prove who, what, where, when and why you are? Everything that is, will you now destroy and uncreate it, times a godzillion? Right and wrong, good and bad, POD and POC, all 100, shorts, boys, POVADs, creations, bases and beyonds.*

When you base your identity and how you fit into the world on how you react to things, both to yourself and to others, any role you take on becomes more about reacting than being truly yourself. Whether you're seen as clever, a troublemaker, or a problem solver, taking on these roles usually means reacting to situations rather than acting from your true self.

Similarly, many people think their personalities are set in stone, sticking to the labels they were given when they were younger. For example, if people always called someone "the angry one," that person might start to believe it and act that way for a long time. Think back to what people thought of you when you were growing up and how you reacted to those opinions. Did you fight against them or start to believe them, shaping who you are now?

> *How many needs of reactive realities do you have to create your personality? Everything that is, will you now destroy and uncreate it, times a godzillion? Right and wrong, good and bad, POD and POC, all 100, shorts, boys, POVADs, creations, bases and beyonds.*

When someone forms an opinion or judgment about you, what's your usual response? Do you react, or do you simply accept it? For most people, reacting is automatic; they don't stop to even consider for a moment that they have another choice. But what if reacting isn't the only option?

Instead of reacting defensively, you could choose to respond differently. You might laugh it off, find enjoyment in it, or simply accept their opinion of you without letting it affect you. Have you ever thought it possible that when people judge you, they might in fact be acknowledging your greatness and power?

Many people believe that judgments restrict them, but that's only true if they react to them. Each time you react to a judgment, you give it more power and make it more significant. However, if you choose not to react and instead see it as a gift, it can empower you.

People tend to judge those they perceive as more powerful than themselves. Their judgments can be seen as attempts to diminish that power. True strength lies in not reacting but in being in allowance of everything that comes your way with openness and grace.

When I was invited for an interview on Swedish national television, I was excited but apprehensive at the same time. I couldn't shake the feeling that the journalist's intentions weren't entirely pure. And as it turned out, my instincts were right.

When the show aired, it was clear they had manipulated my words to fit their narrative. Anger, disappointment, and fear flooded over me followed by a shift in perspective. Then I remembered that every judgment, every criticism, is a gift in disguise. It led me to ask: what contribution could this be to me, my life and my future if I receive it?

As the anticipated the wave of hate emails I expected to trickle in, I was surprised to find only one. The irony wasn't lost on me—the sheer dedication someone had to express their disdain was almost comical. Yet, amidst the negativity, messages of gratitude poured in for the work I do with Pragmatic Psychology.

But the story doesn't end there. The deceitful journalist faced consequences for his actions, losing his job. The show, tainted by dishonesty, was swiftly pulled - never to return.

In hindsight, I realized that power doesn't lie in resistance, but in allowance. Allowance means to not agree or align, nor to resist and react. Adversity doesn't break us; it fuels our ascent to greater heights. And armed with this realization, I continue to soar, undeterred by the storms that may come my way.

> *How many needs of reactive realities are you using to prove that you are subject to other people's points of view and judgments? Everything that is, will you now destroy and uncreate it, times a godzillion? Right and wrong, good and bad, POD and POC, all 100, shorts, boys, POVADs, creations, bases and beyonds.*

CHAPTER 5

Relationships...
From Cage to Creation

In the world, many see relationships as a world of reactions. Initially, it might be about joy, but soon it becomes about fulfilling personal needs and controlling the other person's reactions. Instead of creating together, it's about getting what one wants from the other.

> *How many needs of reactive realities are you using to create the relationships you are choosing? Everything that is, will you now destroy and uncreate it, times a godzillion? Right and wrong, good and bad, POD and POC, all 100, shorts, boys, POVADs, creations, bases and beyonds.*

Imagine if your relationships were not based on needs. Instead of thinking, "How can I make this person do what I want?" you'd ask, "What can I give and receive from this person today?" Having people in your life would be about contributing to each other's growth and happiness. But this takes practice.

We've been taught by our parents and grandparents that relationships are a necessity, that without them, we're not enough. But do you really need someone, or can you choose them? Need creates a sense of lack, while choice creates possibilities.

Think about the people you've decided you need in your life and now question that need. Are you chosen by them, or are you choosing them? Being chosen by others is common, but when you actively choose someone, you have more freedom and control.

Who would be a good fit for you? Who would you enjoy having around? Once you're clear on that, you can actively choose who you want in your life instead of waiting to be chosen.

Years ago, I was content being single but wanted more companionship. I didn't want a traditional relationship; I wanted playmates who would enrich my life and vice versa. Then, unexpectedly, I met a captivating man. Initially, I thought it would just be a casual fling, but it turned into something much deeper. We enjoyed each other's company and discovered a profound connection. Despite our initial intentions to keep things casual, we found ourselves drawn to each other. Our past experiences with relationships made us wary, but our bond was undeniable.

After a few weeks, he called me and suggested meeting up. I paused and asked myself, "What would meeting at this time create?" It felt light and expansive, so I agreed. We met, had wonderful conversations, enjoyed each other's company, and then parted ways with no plan to meet again. This pattern continued for about nine months, and it was a delightful experience. We allowed each other space to be joyful together, without any expectations or labels on our connection.

After nine months, we felt it was time to make a different choice. We asked ourselves, "What future could we create by having each other in our lives even more?" We felt the lightness of that choice, and from then on, we approached our relationship without reacting to the past.

Key elements of our dynamic included trusting ourselves, allowing space for each other, gratitude, honor, humor, vulnerability, choosing rather than needing, and letting go of past patterns.

Relationships often begin with a desire for intimacy, but when expectations and judgments take over, distance can grow. By shifting from a need to a choice, we can cultivate a "creationship" rather than a relationship where we continually seek ways to enhance each other's lives. A creationship is a dynamic space where both individuals consciously contribute to growth, possibilities, and mutual empowerment, free from rigid expectations

How many assumptions do you have about your role in relationships? Do you believe you have to fix or make your partner happy? It can be challenging to witness the suffering of those we care about, but it's important to approach these situations with openness and empathy.

How often do you sacrifice your own happiness for your partner's mood? Does giving up yourself make your partner happier? What if you could accept your partner's choices, even if they're unhappy or suffering?

If you can't accept their choice to suffer, you end up reacting to their assumptions and trying to control them into choosing differently. But that's exhausting! When your partner is in pain, rejects money, or makes choices that limit them, what's your response?

> *Right and wrong, good and bad, POD and POC, all 100, shorts, boys, POVADs, creations, bases and beyonds.*

How many needs of reactive realities are you using to make yourself less than you are as a way to get an appropriate reaction from others? Everything that is, will you now destroy and uncreate it, times a godzillion? Right and wrong, good and bad, POD and POC, all 100, shorts, boys, POVADs, creations, bases and beyonds.

Often, our immediate reaction to someone's suffering is to diminish ourselves to help them. But making ourselves smaller doesn't truly assist anyone. Embracing our full selves, with joy and ease, is what inspires greatness in others. Recognize that you are a gift, just as you are.

When I work with clients who have experienced abuse, I don't shrink myself to fit their suffering. Instead, I remain true to myself, and clients often find it refreshing and liberating. They realize they have choices beyond their pain. When you shrink during hard times, it makes you feel like a victim. But staying true to yourself when things are tough is a big gift. Your happiness, humor, and lightness show others that they can be light too, even if they are not ready. You are not in charge of what others do; helping them make choices, even if it's hard, is real empowerment.

Once, while working with a group of parents, some of whom were homeschooling their children, empowering them to learn in their unique way. However, their spouses were skeptical, clinging to the idea of traditional schooling. The parents felt the need to explain and justify their approach to their partners, but I encouraged them to recognize the gift they were to their children.

We explored the future they were creating for their children with their unconventional parenting style. As they acknowledged their greatness, they became more confident, and their partners relaxed. It wasn't about explaining anymore; it was about knowing their worth and leading by example. People often believe that worrying is a form of control, but it's just another reactive response.

We have been conditioned to rely on presumptive realities and the needs of reactive realities as our life's GPS. They tend to dictate what we should choose, what's right, what's appropriate, and how to react in every situation. But does this genuinely match who you are or are you continually striving to meet these external expectations, relinquishing control of your life instead of shaping it?

The real GPS in life is your knowing, sometimes called intuition or inner voice which leads you towards what is congruent with your very being. When your choices are congruent with who you are, the path to a fulfilling life unfolds effortlessly. Being congruent means your choices reflect you with everything you truly are. For instance, if you ask for more money just because others do, but it doesn't truly bring you joy, you're not congruent with that ask. But if asking for more money genuinely brings happiness and expands your world, then you're in alignment with that request.

Many people tend to ask for things based on image rather than genuine fulfillment. They prioritize what looks good to others over what truly brings them happiness.

> *How many presumptive realties and needs of reactive realities do you have about what you should ask for and what should make you happy that keeps you from creating a wonderful life that uniquely works for you? Everything that is, will you now destroy and uncreate it, times a godzillion? Right and wrong, good and bad, POD and POC, all 100, shorts, boys, POVADs, creations, bases and beyonds.*

Many people unknowingly create their lives within a gilded cage, chasing after a dream that isn't truly theirs. Pursuing a life that merely looks good on the outside is a form of self-sabotage, detrimental to both body and spirit. Have you noticed how those leading seemingly perfect lives often age rapidly or turn to drugs? What appears as freedom soon becomes a confining cage, adorned with superficiality.

The allure of appearances is a potent force for destruction. Reflect on your own life: where do you conform to societal standards, and at what cost? How much energy do you expend against yourself to maintain this façade?

Your judgments are the sole barrier between you and true freedom, ease, joy, and glory. And in this case. I'm referring to glory as the exuberant expression and abundance of life. Imagine embracing what truly makes you happy, regardless of how it may appear to others. By doing so, you become an inspiration, a trendsetter, a new leader.

Consider the journey of Forrest Gump, who starts as an outsider but evolves into a beloved celebrity. His choices are simply congruent with who he is; there's no need for grandiosity or significance. He embraces what works for him and moves forward, welcoming each new adventure.

This is an invitation to lead your life beyond the confines of perfection, embracing ease and joy and glory. Should you see past experiences what new possibilities and insights might you gain?

Recently, my partner and I were in the market for a new car. Despite societal expectations, we opted for a vehicle that truly resonated with us—a stunning peacock blue car with all the features we desired. This unconventional choice brought us immense joy and gratitude, demonstrating that fulfillment transcends societal norms.

Instead of striving for perfection, embrace change and ask yourself, "What else is possible? How can it get even better?" By relinquishing the need for perfection, you open yourself up to unexpected possibilities and growth.

In the past, I always flew economy class content with the simplicity it offered. Despite multiple offers to upgrade, I resisted, clinging to my presumptive reality. However, after questioning my resistance and considering the future, I chose to upgrade. This decision not only provided comfort but also transformed my financial reality. By aligning my choices with what truly nurtured me, I attracted greater abundance into my life.

Similarly, I once assumed I wanted children because of societal pressure. However, after seeking clarity, I realized that motherhood wasn't congruent with my desires. Embracing this truth brought relaxation and freedom. Yet, when my partner's daughter expressed a desire for me to be her mother. I explored what motherhood could be leading to wonderful new possibilities for all of us. When you start creating your life and enjoying yourself more, some people may feel uncomfortable with your freedom. They might project their insecurities onto you, making you question your happiness or success. In those moments, pause and recognize what's happening. Instead of falling back into old patterns to please them, choose again to prioritize ease and joy.

The presumptive realities and reactive needs of society often highlight what's wrong rather than celebrating your greatness. How much energy do you spend obsessing over what's not working, hoping it will eventually change? What if you are not flawed? Reflect on the strategies you have learnt from your upbringing or culture to handle challenges—do you react or take proactive steps?

Acknowledging the greatness of what you've already created empowers you to pursue even more from a place of relaxation rather than reaction. Consider your life: what if nothing is inherently wrong? What if even the challenges you face are opportunities for growth and magic? Embracing every aspect of your life as a gift frees you from the shackles of judgment.

How many needs of reactive realities and presumptive realities do you hold onto, constantly judging yourself and your life? It's time to release them all. Let's dissolve these limitations: Everything that is, will you now destroy and uncreate it, times a godzillion? Right and wrong, good and bad, POD and POC, all 100, shorts, boys, POVADs, creations, bases and beyonds.

Chapter 6

Let the Games Begin

If your actions weren't driven by necessity, what would you genuinely seek in your life? Engaging solely with reactive and presumptive realities prevents you from discerning your true desires. Your options become limited to conforming to others' expectations, societal norms, and appearances. Basically, you're just making your captivity look nicer. Is that sufficient for you? What more do you genuinely crave? By going beyond these reactive and presumptive states, you can attain clarity about what truly resonates with you and who you truly are.

What is true for you?

I have the privilege of knowing a remarkable gardener who tends to a breathtaking sanctuary in Costa Rica. His connection with the plants transcends mere caretaking; he perceives them as beloved companions. He engages in conversations with them, nurturing them back to health when they falter. His contentment is palpable, rooted in the profound truth he embodies.

In a world obsessed with conventional notions of success, some may view his life as modest, perhaps even insignificant. Yet, such judgments are not relevant to him. He understands his truth and pursues what he loves relentlessly. In doing so, he becomes a beacon of inspiration not only to the flora under his care but to the very Earth itself. Can you fathom the immense gift someone like him is to our world? His joy, his gratitude for every living thing, creates ripples of magnificence that reverberate across continents.

Consider the expansiveness of his existence. Likewise, reflect on your own. Do you recognize the gift you are simply by being and choosing what is true for you? When we embrace genuineness and find happiness in our existence, we emit a radiant energy that touches the world around us.

We often tend to underestimate the profound impact of living a life that is congruent with our being. When we embrace who we truly are and find happiness in our existence, we emit a radiant energy that touches the world around us.

Consider this: there's no universal measure for the size or significance of a life. Whether it is labeled as small or large by societal standards is irrelevant. What truly matters is what makes you happy. If a modest life brings you joy, revel in it. On the other hand, if you aspire towards wealth and grandeur beyond societal norms, pursue it with enthusiasm.

Take a moment to reflect: What truly matters to you? What fills your heart with space and joy? Free yourself from comparisons to others and envision the greatness that resonates with your soul.

The essence of action lies not in the deed itself but in the space from which it originates. Instead of seeking the 'right' action driven by judgment, where one weighs what is deemed correct or incorrect, focus on what serves your well-being.

Reflect on this scenario: Two people achieve financial success, but for different reasons. One seeks social approval and the appearance of success, while the other finds joy and fulfillment in creativity. Despite similar outcomes, their motivations are different. This shows that the essence of our actions goes beyond appearances. What drives you: the need for external validation or the genuine happiness of living genuinely?

CHAPTER 7

Choice… the Beginning of New Adventures

Imagine a world where the need to be right or perfect, and the reliance on others, fades away. From this space, what choices would you embrace, and who would you become? Need, born from the illusion of lack, perpetuates a ceaseless quest for external validation—be it in resources, time, or relationships. It stands as one of the greatest deceptions woven into the fabric of human consciousness. Consider this: When engulfed by a sense of need, does it resonate with who you truly are? Or does it burden you with heaviness? Your truth always lifts you, while falsehoods weigh you down.

How many presumptive realities have you bought as real, telling you that need is real and that you have no other choice than constantly having lack in your life? Everything that is, will you now destroy and uncreate it, times a godzillion? Right and wrong, good and bad, POD and POC, all 100, shorts, boys, POVADs, creations, bases and beyonds.

Let's delve into the notion of choice. While many have heard about having the power to choose, few truly grasp the depth of choice available in every moment of our lives. A common belief persists that our past and present experiences dictate our paths, thereby constraining our ability to exercise complete freedom of choice.

Yet, it's crucial to recognize that our reality is shaped by our point of view If we believe that past traumas or challenges like abuse or divorce constrain our future possibilities, then indeed, we manifest those limitations.

Never underestimate the potency of your viewpoints. When you hold onto beliefs like 'I can't surpass my family's financial status,' you inadvertently filter out opportunities that seek to enrich your life. Similarly, observe how you can often identify choices that could vastly improve the lives of others, yet they remain blind to them due to their entrenched viewpoints. Now, turn the lens inward. Reflect upon this question: "Where do my own points of view obscure my vision, hindering the multitude of possibilities and choices available to me?"

To practice choice, set aside preconceptions and explore various facets of your life—money, body, career, relationships—and inquire, 'What choices lie here that I've yet to acknowledge? What else could I choose?'

When grappling with decisions, such as whether to stay in a job or relationship, resist the trap of reactive thinking. 'Either-or' scenarios merely offer a 50/50 chance, devoid of true choice. Instead of seeking a conclusion or presumptive reality, ponder the futures each option presents. Ask, 'What future unfolds if I stay? What unfolds if I leave?' Avoid the illusion of a 'right' or 'wrong' choice, for every choice holds potential. By focusing on the future each choice creates, we invite awareness, transcending the limitations of reactive thinking.

Choice transcends judgment. Embrace the vast array of futures awaiting your selection. What future will you choose to create?

A profound realization is that there is no inherently right or wrong future. In our world, we're wired to judge whether things are good or bad. Have you ever noticed how much mental energy we spend on deciding if something is good or bad?

How about dedicating one day, or even starting with half a day, to consciously observing how frequently you find yourself assessing whether you, others, or situations are good or bad, right or wrong? How else you could utilize your energy if it weren't consumed by judgments throughout the day? When we embark on a journey of creating our lives through questions and choices, rather than conclusions and judgments, it truly is an adventure.

True choice comes from no judgement.

What if you knew that you have a choice in every single moment of every day to create a life that is great for you? Practice choice! Right now, in this very moment, what would you like to choose? Keep on reading? Just sitting in your chair and enjoying being, looking out the window, being grateful… what else? There are so many choices available in every moment of our lives. Now what would you like to choose next? It takes practice to choose after being used to reacting all the time. Need is a reaction to what shows up in the moment. Choice is where you create your life. Once you choose, you oversee your life.

Chapter 8

When Your Body Is No Longer Your Cage

Consider this: Have you ever viewed your body as akin to nature itself—an entity devoid of judgment, point of view, or choice, operating effortlessly in each moment? Much like the Earth and its natural inhabitants, your body functions from a state of being, not from reactive needs.

Your body works effortlessly when you are in a natural state of being. Yet, how often do you strive for the "right" reaction from your body? How frequently do you find yourself grappling with what to do to elicit a specific response from your body?

Trying to force your body into conformity through methods such as dieting or intense workouts is akin to seeking a specific reaction. But does this method yield genuine results? Your body flourishes when approached with inquiries, not demands.

Instead, engage in a dialogue with your body. Inquire about its desires, its ideal appearance, and its needs to achieve the size it desires. Your body holds the answers, but these insights remain elusive as long as presumptive realities cloud your perception.

> *How many needs of reactive realities and presumptive realities are you using to try to create a difference with your body are you choosing? Everything that is, will you now destroy and uncreate it, times a godzillion? Right and wrong, good and bad, POD and POC, all 100, shorts, boys, POVADs, creations, bases and beyonds.*

How many presumptions do you hold about your weight, believing it's solely influenced by your diet and actions? These assumptions arise from reactive needs, aiming to manipulate your body to meet your desires, rather than fostering a cooperative connection with it.

How many needs or reactive realities and presumptive realities are you using to determine the weight of your body are you choosing? Everything that is, will you now destroy and uncreate it, times a godzillion? Right and wrong, good and bad, POD and POC, all 100, shorts, boys, POVADs, creations, bases and beyonds.

Change can feel almost magical when you truly listen to your body instead of assuming. Ask your body what it needs for change and let it guide you without stress. How often do you expect instant results and then try to force things to happen by controlling every situation? It's exhausting! Isn't there an easier way? Presuming and controlling won't truly create the life you want.

Do you often try to impose your desires onto situations or people, then work hard to make them happen? Would you prefer a simpler approach? Try receiving instead of controlling!

Facilitating change in your body or any aspect of life begins with asking for the change and then embracing it without the pressure of perfection. Receiving doesn't demand effort; when you ask for change, you've already set its actualization in motion. It's on its way.

As you ask for what you desire, remain open to what else might be needed for it to actualize. If you seek change within your body, it will gently signal what adjustments are required. You may find yourself drawn to a store or product seemingly without reason; follow what feels light and uplifting for both you and your body, rather than what feels burdensome. If someone's advice on weight loss feels restrictive and contracts your world, it may not align with your body's needs.

Others' opinions are merely perspectives, but what truly matters is what resonates as true for you. What is true for you brings a sense of lightness, while falsehoods weigh heavily. Your body thrives on playfulness and ease, much like children and animals. Engaging in activities that bring joy and lightness triggers the vital energy of aliveness—a generative force used by all living beings, including the Earth, to create change and progress forward.

Chapter 9

Pain

By choosing to remain within the confines of your gilded cage, exerting control over your life and resisting change, you inadvertently foster stagnation, stuckness, and contraction both in your life and within your body. This stagnant state is often the breeding ground for various forms of pain, whether physical or emotional, leading to feelings of frustration and discontent.

> *How many pains in your body are based on needs of reactive realties? Everything that is, will you now destroy and uncreate it, times a godzillion? Right and wrong, good and bad, POD and POC, all 100, shorts, boys, POVADs, creations, bases and beyonds.*

When faced with a new situation, how do you respond? Do you greet it with gratitude, or do you immediately assess it as good or bad and search for ways to react and control it? Opting for control rather than allowance leads to pain. Trying to bring order to chaos hinders the progress needed for personal growth and development in life.

Years ago, after a surgery, people were advising me to remain still to aid healing. Nowadays, there's a new understanding. Take, for instance, our 84-year-old friend who underwent hip surgery. Just hours after the procedure, she chose to get up and move—and it proved beneficial. She's now pain-free.

Avoiding movement or trying to cope with pain by staying still only exacerbates the discomfort. Embracing movement allows you to tap into the energy trapped within the pain, releasing it and harnessing it to enhance not just your physical well-being but your overall life.

How often have you experienced frustration in life and realized later that it served as a signal for necessary change and progression? If you would allow pain to gift you valuable information, pointing you towards new possibilities, would you need to be triggered with reactive responses?

Consider this: What you perceive as pain may actually be your awareness of others. How much of what you identify as your thoughts, feelings, emotions, and pains stem from your awareness of others' experiences? We often underestimate our level of awareness. Have you ever sensed when someone is feeling down without them saying a word? That's your awareness at work.

How much information do you constantly absorb from your surroundings, often without realizing it? This is why it's crucial to ask, "Who does this belong to? Is this feeling or thought truly mine, or am I picking up on someone else's experience?" By questioning, you can recognize how much you've internalized that doesn't belong to you. How many problems and pains are you carrying that aren't yours to bear? Particularly if you've endured a pain or problem for an extended period despite trying various solutions without success, chances are it's not yours to resolve. What isn't yours, you cannot change.

I've encountered numerous patients who approached me with pains and issues, only to discover that they were carrying someone else's burdens. Upon recognizing this, they experienced a significant lightening of their emotional load, making room for positive change to occur.

How much pain are you carrying for others? Does it work?

How much of the pain in your body and your life is not even yours?

When you carry someone else's pain, you inadvertently rob them of their opportunity to address it themselves. How often have you noticed that as you bear someone else's burden, your own pain intensifies while theirs persists? Many individuals strongly identify with their pain, viewing it as integral to their identity. By relieving them of what they perceive as a defining aspect of themselves, you may inadvertently evoke resistance or frustration. The most significant gift you can offer is to simply allow them to make their own choices. Taking on others' pain only serves to disempower them, whereas granting them the freedom to choose whether to embrace pain or release it empowers them to reclaim agency over their own lives.

How often do you react to fulfill the needs of others? Has your life become a series of reactions aimed at making others' needs about you, rather than about them, all to prove your care?

Pain serves as a means for many individuals to inject intensity into their lives, believing it provides them with a sense of purpose and vitality. They cling to pain as a form of motivation to keep moving forward. Does this rationale truly make sense? Not really, but people seldom make sense.

How many needs of reactive realities are you using to create enough intensity to feel that you are alive? Everything that is, will you now destroy and uncreate it, times a godzillion? Right and wrong, good and bad, POD and POC, all 100, shorts, boys, POVADs, creations, bases and beyonds.

Being a Healer

A healer possesses the ability to create change in people's lives and bodies. It's a remarkable gift, provided one doesn't shy away from or judge it. However, if you believe that being a healer entails shouldering others' pains and suffering, you might perceive it as a burden and attempt to evade your innate abilities.

Consider the possibility of finding ease in embracing your role as a healer. Avoidance inevitably leads to pain. When you neglect your inherent abilities, the only option left is to inadvertently wield them against yourself and your well-being.

Avoidance often generates more pain than receiving does. This is a common misconception for many individuals. They believe that avoidance leads to greater ease, when in reality, it's receiving that fosters more comfort. When you avoid, you erect barriers to distance yourself from undesired experiences. Alternatively, receiving involves allowing things to flow through you.

Healing abilities let you sense how others feel and what's happening in their bodies and lives. You don't have to act on this awareness, but you can. Trying to heal those who don't want it doesn't help anyone. Instead, focus on helping those who are open to it. If you feel your body or mood changing negatively, ask yourself, "Is this from someone else?" If yes, check if they want healing. If not, stop and let it go.

Questioning if the pain was mine, I would undergo healing processes without even being aware of it. However, during shared accommodations on trips, I struggled to sleep, and my physical well-being suffered without explanation. Once I started asking myself, "Is this discomfort mine? Is it related to the person next to me and their physical state that I'm sensing? Do they seek my assistance?" More often than not, the answer was "no." At that moment, I would remind myself to stop, and suddenly, ease returned to my body.

We and our bodies possess remarkable, undiscovered abilities. Why not embark on an adventure with your body, inviting it to reveal its capabilities and wisdom?

Your body thrives in unity, connected to everything and everyone. But when you adopt a fixed viewpoint, you separate yourself. Your body follows your lead.

By holding onto a perspective, you limit yourself and create discomfort. Instead, imagine exploring the endless possibilities with your body as your companion.

Ask your body to show you what it knows.

Ask your body to facilitate you to more of what is true for you.

What playmates can you and your body be that you have not yet considered?

Chapter 10

Psychological Cages

When you only see yourself through your thoughts and feelings, you limit yourself to a small space. But beyond that lies a vast realm where you can fully be, know, and perceive everything. Your thoughts and feelings are just part of the picture. How much more of yourself can you uncover beyond them?

Each time you define something, you limit your role in this reality, confining yourself to a fixed identity or expectation. By doing so, you miss out on the freedom to explore the many possibilities and roles you could embody.

How much of yourself are you suppressing to avoid being overwhelming for others? What assumptions have you made about the impact of being your true self on others? When you shift from being fully yourself to holding back, what is your intention? Are you trying to avoid causing discomfort? Have you concluded that your true self may harm others? In truth, what you challenge are not individuals, but rather their limitations. Is this a negative outcome, or rather a testament to your power, making it difficult for others to cling to their constraints in your presence?

How much of depression, anxiety, frustration, and other psychological pain arises from avoiding embracing your true power and potential for making a difference?

What forces pull you back into confinement? Think about those moments when you're truly being yourself and enjoying life. What interrupts that freedom—someone pretending to be hurt, angry, or sad because of you? People often know exactly how to manipulate you into returning to your cage. How often do you fall for it?

When you see things and people as they truly are, not as they wish to appear, you attain freedom. Always inquire: What are the intentions behind the words and actions of those around you? Are they seeking to uplift and empower you, or are they endeavoring to confine you within their own limitations? If it's the latter, remain calm. There is no need to judge or react. Instead, be thankful for your courage to perceive reality and then choose your path. Engaging in judgment and confrontation only amplifies their limitations. By acknowledging what is and moving forward, you go beyond it and inspire others to do the same, thereby creating a greater world.

How much does your definition of "caring" hinder you to be more of you?

Caring

For many, caring revolves around their own needs, wanting others to change to fit their expectations. It's a biased understanding of caring we've adopted. Genuine caring embraces both yourself and others, without exclusion. The crucial element is allowance. You grant others the freedom to change or stay the same, respecting their choices. There's no judgment on whether their choices are right or wrong. Once they choose, it's theirs forever. True caring empowers both yourself and others to discover what's true for each of you.

How about relinquishing the controls in your life that hinder you from reaching the greatness you're capable of?

Stress

Stress is where people prove that they have a life.

> *How many needs of reactive realties are you using to create the stress you are choosing? Everything that is, will you now destroy and uncreate it, times a godzillion? Right and wrong, good and bad, POD and POC, all 100, shorts, boys, POVADs, creations, bases and beyonds.*

Stress often arises as a reaction, a chosen intensity to demonstrate a sense of purpose in life. Have you ever observed how you generate stress even when it's not necessary? If you lived a life filled with ease and joy, would you or others view it as laziness? Consider how much more productive you could be if you approached life from a place of relaxation.

What if you didn't feel the need to manufacture drama, stress, or pain to validate your existence? True living is about choice—actively choosing in every moment.

What could you choose right now… from relaxation?

> *How many presumptive realities and needs of reactive realities do you have creating your body, relationship with your body, relationship with money and everything else in your life?*

Everything that is, will you now destroy and uncreate it, times a godzillion? Right and wrong, good and bad, POD and POC, all 100, shorts, boys, POVADs, creations, bases and beyonds.

How many presumptive realities and needs of reactive realties are you using, thinking that if you do not function from them, you cannot know anything and you have no choice but using them to control everything in your life, rather than being the difference and miracle called you? Everything that is, will you now destroy and uncreate it, times a godzillion? Right and wrong, good and bad, POD and POC, all 100, shorts, boys, POVADs, creations, bases and beyonds.

Do you feel stressed because you have too much going on in your life, or perhaps too little? Creative individuals thrive on the energy derived from their creations. Have you noticed how being in the zone and enjoying your work actually energizes you? Creation adds to your energy—it doesn't drain it. Many believe that reducing activity conserves energy and reduces stress. However, in truth, cutting back because you think you lack energy often makes you feel worse. Your perspective molds your reality.

Many years ago, when I was employed and working for another business, those around me remarked that I seemed overworked, tired, and stressed, suggesting I take a vacation. Convinced that they were right, I took two weeks off and headed to a beachside destination. Prior to my trip, I sought advice on how to alleviate my stress. Much of it revolved around minimizing activity and sleeping extensively. I followed suit, only to find those weeks to be the most depressing, tedious and frustrating of my life. Rather than feeling rejuvenated, I found myself with even less energy. For a creative individual, forcing oneself to do nothing only adds to stress, contradicting our inherent nature. It's a reminder that things aren't always as they seem.

Since then, I've made a different choice. Instead of blindly following others' notions of what's good and right, I began exploring what truly works for me and my body. Many people around us claim to know what's best for us and insist they have the answers, but you're the only one who truly knows what's good for you and your body. Once I started prioritizing what brings more space and ease to me and my body, my entire life, including my business and finances, began to flourish!

Now, my life isn't about balancing work and leisure; it's about constant creation, whether I'm teaching a class or trekking up a mountain.

What if life wasn't about doing less and conserving energy? A mindset rooted in scarcity and ultimately leading to stress. What if your life revolved around the question, "What more can I bring into my life?" purely for the joy of it and the endless possibilities it could bring?

CHAPTER 11

The Ease Consciousness Can Bring

Consciousness is pragmatic. It is about doing what works. Rather than worrying about what is right for others, you get to have clarity about what is good for you, which includes others.

Consciousness is turning on the lights. You get to see what is from no judgement. It gives you clarity on your life and your choices and which one of them create a greater future and which one of them limit your future.

Consciousness includes everything and judges nothing. Ask for it. Ask for more consciousness in your life. Choose more consciousness. There is no "how" to it. The less you are avoiding, the more consciousness you are inviting. The areas of your life that you avoid looking at, you can only function from unconsciousness. This makes it very hard to change anything.

What have you decided avoiding gives you? What have you decided you will win with avoiding? Once you realize that it won't work, you can make a more pragmatic choice. When you see things as they truly are, without judgment or attachment, you gain the freedom to create your life.

Take a moment to examine your life: are there areas where you're unknowingly limiting yourself? Sometimes, we avoid uncomfortable truths, preferring comfort and appearances. But in doing so, we confine ourselves without realizing it.

I recently spoke with a friend who worked as a massage therapist for years, content with a low wage because her employer offered free personal development sessions. Only later did she realize she was being exploited, those sessions keeping her self-doubt alive. When she left, she felt liberated.

Clarity comes in its own time; we can't force it on others. We can only lead by example and let them find their own truth. When they do, they become empowered.

Acknowledging our limitations takes courage. There's no perfect way to do it; it's about choosing to see clearly and letting go of what doesn't make us happy. Instead of judging ourselves, we should celebrate our bravery. Perfection is a myth; by embracing imperfection we explore new possibilities.

Consciousness is pragmatic; it helps us see what works for us. More consciousness brings clarity to our choices, showing us which ones lead to a better future. Avoidance leads to unconsciousness, making change difficult. Once we realize this, we can make smarter choices for growth and awareness.

Gaslighting

While my friend was led to believe that the additional personal development sessions, she received were a valuable bonus, it took a while for her to realize that these sessions weren't meant to empower her but rather to keep her subservient to her employer. She was subjected to gaslighting.

Gaslighting often goes unnoticed initially. The perpetrator may appear well-intentioned, while gradually eroding the victim's confidence and self-trust, making them dependent. My friend felt trapped in her job, convinced she had no alternatives and relied on her boss not just for work but also for life advice. It was only when she reached a breaking point, feeling trapped and unhappy, that she recognized the need for change and began empowering herself to break free from the gilded cage.

Many relationships resemble gilded cages, seemingly ideal from the outside but suffocating within. Surprisingly, studies show that many would rather endure a bad or abusive relationship than be alone. This speaks volumes about societal norms—suffering is accepted as normal. How willing are you to break free and prioritize your own happiness?

Consider the dynamics of your relationships. Who do you believe you need? If you shed light on the situation, what truths would emerge? Is the dependency mutual, or are you being manipulated into believing you need someone?

Gaslighting is a form of abuse that erodes self-trust, leaving victims vulnerable and dependent. People who gaslight aim to convince you that you're ignorant or mentally unstable. Those who seek to disempower others do so to assert dominance. Their belief is rooted in the notion that their power is derived from diminishing others. When you refuse to engage in their manipulation, you reclaim your freedom.

Trust in yourself and your intuition; refuse to accept the false narrative imposed upon you. Empower yourself by repeatedly asking, "What is true for me in this situation? What knowledge am I suppressing?" Truth brings clarity and lightness, while falsehoods weigh you down.

How many times have you allowed yourself to be gaslit? There's no need for self-judgment; acknowledge your courage in recognizing past choices and empower yourself to make new ones.

Whom can you release from your inner circle? Whom can you welcome into your life, fostering growth and well-being? What mindset must you adopt to embody an invitation to possibilities that amplify your greatness?

Adapting to others' expectations often comes with a heavy cost. What sacrifices are you making to dwell within the ornate cages crafted by others?

Breaking free may initially evoke discomfort, and the path forward might appear unclear, but it marks the beginning of embracing more of your true self and unlocking levels of freedom beyond imagination. How kind can you be towards yourself? How much more can you prioritize your own well-being and involvement in your life's decisions? How many false beliefs have you internalized, convincing yourself that prioritizing self-care and nurturing your needs makes you selfish or egotistical? Is that truly the case?

Often, those who accuse others of selfishness reflect their own behaviors. Consider the individuals who label you as egotistical or self-centered—how do they treat those around them? Who truly embodies egotism: you or them? Embrace reality, and you will be free.

Striving for change and seeking greater freedom and ease in your life can unsettle others because it challenges the validity of their own limitations and the confines of their gilded cages. Take this reaction as a compliment; It signifies your evolution and your journey toward becoming more genuine. You may come to realize that some individuals you once considered friends were only supportive as long as you conformed to their way of life, shared their perspectives, judgments, and presumed realities, and adhered to reactive needs.

Celebrate your uniqueness as a blessing, not a flaw. Imagine viewing your differences as miracles rather than obstacles. Diversity propels progress, while uniformity preserves the status quo. Which path would you prefer to follow? Many social circles are built upon conformity. Whether it is friendships, cultural groups, or shared viewpoints, these communities often adhere to fixed realities and expect members to respond in a certain way. When you deviate from the group's consensus or resist their expectations, your belonging within that group may be jeopardized.

Have you ever experienced a moment when you felt uncertain or neutral, only to be criticized for not taking a definitive stance? The pressure to conform to societal norms often dictates that to be considered "real," one must align with prevailing viewpoints—even if it means conforming to the restrictive norms of the gilded cage in which many reside. But why not be true to yourself instead?

Instead of conforming to others' expectations, embrace your true self and create a reality that resonates with you.

Years ago, I asked a close friend how he met his partner. Together, they radiated creativity, constantly innovating and inspiring others with their collaborative ventures.

His response struck me: "Before finding this person, I was content being alone with my thoughts and ideas. I realized I had fabricated a need for someone to complete my world. Once I recognized this perspective, I released it. Instead, I embraced solitude, reveling in the wonders of life from that space. It was liberating—no expectations, just pure being and receiving. The world itself became the partner I thought I lacked. Soon after, I encountered a remarkable man who perfectly aligned with my desires. Our union was born from contribution, not dependency. The key to receiving was learning to receive myself."

What needs of belonging are you inventing that keeps you from being and enjoying you? Everything that is, will you now destroy and uncreate it, times a godzillion? Right and wrong, good and bad, POD and POC, all 100, shorts, boys, POVADs, creations, bases and beyonds.

Who are your potential playmates at this moment? Playfulness is a dynamic force that facilitates change at any moment. Unlike rigid relationships, a playmate doesn't demand you to conform or remain static. They appreciate you for who you are, operating from a place of joy and levity, reigniting the spark of life within you that you may have forgotten existed—and vice versa.

Doesn't that feel markedly different from clinging to someone simply because they've been in your life for some time, especially if their presence leaves you feeling diminished? Always remember, you have the power of choice—always!

Have you concluded that what you currently have is as good as it gets?

How many presumptive realities do you have telling you that what you have is all you can get and holding on to it is your only choice? Everything that is, will you now destroy and uncreate it, times a godzillion? Right and wrong, good and bad, POD and POC, all 100, shorts, boys, POVADs, creations, bases and beyonds.

This falsehood is one of the most deeply ingrained beliefs people accept as truth. It keeps them stuck in their current circumstances, preventing them from seeking more and rising above their limits. How thoroughly have you embraced the notion that what you currently possess represents the extent of what's available to you? Instead, reflect on the countless instances in your life where letting go of people or things that no longer nurtured you resulted in profound personal growth and an expanded life experience.

Take a moment to observe your surroundings. How many items in your home do you hold onto despite no longer finding joy or purpose in them? Here's a simple experiment: select one item and let it go. Notice the shift it brings. Do you feel a sense of relaxation? Does it create more physical or mental space for you? Do you experience a newfound sense of freedom? What often escapes our awareness is that retaining possessions that no longer bring us joy exacts a toll greater than we realize.

While the cost may not be monetary, there's an energetic expense involved. When we release belongings and relationships that no longer nurture us, we liberate the energy previously bound up in maintaining them, allowing it to flow freely once again.

Take a comprehensive look around: within your home, your relationships, the services you utilize for internet platforms, phone services, files on your computer, and all other aspects of your life. Identify what you continue to invest in, whether it's financially, emotionally, or energetically, that if released, would create room for new and greater possibilities to emerge.

Chapter 12

What Is Next in Your Life?

Consider the scope of your choices: Is your menu limited to what others dictate as possible? Restricted to what you've previously selected? Or is it as expansive as you permit it to be? What if you didn't require full comprehension of all possibilities before pursuing something new and greater?

When I started my first business, I maintained my employment for the perceived security of a steady income. A friend's probing question challenged this perspective: "What is the true cost of holding onto that belief?" This inquiry shook me to my core. She continued, "Is it time to release your job and fully invest in your business? How much potential revenue could you generate?" It dawned on me that my reluctance stemmed from an inability to envision the future success of my business. Instead of waiting for certainty, I chose to actively shape my destiny. Embracing the unknown, I leapt into entrepreneurship—and was astounded by the abundance that unfolded before me.

Creating change isn't merely about tweaking the elements of your life—it's not about redecorating the cage you've constructed. True change involves transcending the confines of the box you've labeled your life thus far and daring to leap into the unknown.

> *How many presumptive realties do you have about what it means to jump into the unknown? Everything that is, will you now destroy and uncreate it, times a godzillion? Right and wrong, good and bad, POD and POC, all 100, shorts, boys, POVADs, creations, bases and beyonds.*

Reading a book about overcoming limitations suggests a curiosity about what lies beyond the current boundaries and a yearning for growth. If you were content with things as they are, you might not have bothered. It's like asking yourself if you're ready to try something new and to explore what else life has to offer. It poses the question of whether now the opportune moment is to embark on a new journey of self-discovery and fulfillment.

As you set out on a new path, do you pause to contemplate how the changes might materialize and what form they might take? It's like expanding the boundaries of a box, pushing its limits while still recognizing its existence. But what if you dared to explore beyond these boundaries? What if you could sculpt your life and future without being constrained by any preconceptions? What else is possible?

> *How many presumptive realties and needs of reactive realties are you using to get a clue on how to navigate your life when all you do is control your life into smallness? Everything that is, will you now destroy and uncreate it, times a godzillion? Right and wrong, good and bad, POD and POC, all 100, shorts, boys, POVADs, creations, bases and beyonds.*

Presumptions may appear as reliable guides, offering a clear path to success. Yet, they often confine us to smaller visions of what's possible. Stepping beyond these assumptions can initially leave us feeling adrift, as if we've lost our way. However, this discomfort signals a crucial shift—a departure from limiting beliefs toward expansive potential. Embrace this moment of uncertainty as a sign of progress. Rather than seeking control or understanding, allow yourself to surrender to the mysteries of the unknown. It's in this space of openness that true growth thrives. Congratulations on venturing into uncharted territory—keep moving forward with courage and curiosity.

When you are accepted, what will you have achieved? Is it the approval of others, or is it your own inner acceptance that truly matters? Often, we seek validation from the outside, yet the deepest fulfillment comes from embracing ourselves fully, without needing external confirmation. Acceptance from within allows us to live authentically, regardless of the opinions or judgments of others.

Who or what is the driving force behind the creation of your life? As you select your clothes each morning, is it primarily for your own satisfaction or to meet the expectations of others? In your conversations, do you carefully select your words to please others, or do you say what is true for you? When deciding how to spend your time each day, whose desires are you prioritizing?

What guides your decisions: your being or the expectations imposed by others? Who do you see when you look beyond the roles society assigns you? And perhaps more importantly, who could you become if you dared to transcend those limitations?

How much of who you truly are must you sacrifice to conform to the allure of the gilded cage? While it may initially feel like relinquishing your identity and autonomy, consider what waits beyond those gilded bars. How much of your true self must you silence to meet society's standards of perfection? Can royalty truly find their voice and freedom within the confines of their constructed empire, or are they ensnared by the illusion of perfection they've meticulously crafted? Pause and reflect: are you chasing after appearances, or are you prioritizing genuine happiness and fulfillment?

Fairy tales typically conclude neatly, leaving little room for further exploration or evolution. Persistently chasing the fantasy of a fairy tale or an idealized image can prevent genuine self-expression and fulfillment. Who are you shaping yourself to become, and whose standards are you striving to meet? In numerous relationships, partners may harbor preconceived notions, expecting each other to fit into predetermined molds like perfect accessories. Are you reducing yourself to merely being someone's ideal adornment? In your earnest attempts to fulfill their wishes and meet their expectations, can you still discern the resonance of your own voice? How many of your own treasures have you relinquished along the way to seamlessly integrate into someone else's world?

A friend of mine married a very wealthy man. She is a beautiful, intelligent, and creative woman, and everyone was thrilled when she announced the wedding. Friends and family exclaimed, "What a perfect man! You'll be so well taken care of. You'll never have to worry about a thing. You'll have everything. You're so lucky." It's funny how people suddenly believe they can predict the future. They were mistaken. Despite having everything that one might think brings happiness, she fell into a deep depression and started drinking. No one understood what had happened. In their eyes, she had seemingly ruined the most perfect life anyone could imagine. She faced shame, judgment, and vilification.

To be with her husband, she had to sacrifice much of her life, her joys, and her very being. The circle of her husband's friends, his image, family, and lifestyle demanded she give up herself. For a while, she tried hard to meet everyone's expectations, to make it work, to compromise. But eventually, she realized the price was too high. The perfect gilded life cost her herself.

Then, she made a brave new choice. She let go of what no one is ever supposed to let go of, and what she gained was immeasurable. She reclaimed her life, her joy, and her being. In doing so, she found a happiness and fulfillment far beyond what anyone had ever predicted.

People often focus on what they can gain, overlooking the abundance they already possess. What do you have that you seldom or never acknowledge? Imagine if you stopped judging these blessings as not enough or not good enough. Starting with gratitude can lead you to even greater wealth.

Are you trying to shield yourself from others' needs and judgments? Are you hiding behind walls you've built, ensuring no one sees or hurts you? These walls keep out everything, including the nurturing that can help you and your life grow. As long as you make your life about seeking acceptance and approval, what will you have achieved at the end of the day? Is that truly enough for you?

Embrace gratitude and let down your walls. Allow yourself to be seen and nurtured, and discover the true richness life has to offer.

CHAPTER 13

What Does It Take To Cure the Gilded Cage?

Turn on the Lights

As you journey through this book, you might have realized that true change comes from seeing things as they are. Turning on the lights means becoming aware of where you are in your life, identifying what parts are working for you, and acknowledging what parts are not. This requires courage, vulnerability, and a willingness to let go of the need to always be right.

Do You Need to Be Right?

If you strive to be right, you are merely decorating your limitations. Rightness is not a worthwhile destination. Instead, consider setting your course towards "choice."

Choice Creates

Choice is never about being right or wrong. Every choice creates a different path. By choosing rather than waiting to get it right, you can move your life forward. To overcome the need for correctness and the stress of doubt, simply ask yourself, "If I make this choice, what future will it create? If I make the other choice, what future will that create?" Instead of overanalyzing, go with what feels lighter and creates more space and relaxation in your life. You possess an innate knowing that goes beyond mere thinking.

What Do You Know?

When you are done overthinking and start feeling bored with yourself, begin to ask for what you already know. Thinking often tries to control the situation, while knowing helps you navigate your life towards greatness.

Ask yourself, "What do I already know about this that I am pretending not to know?

Do you sense how others are feeling without them telling you? Do you sometimes anticipate events before they happen? Do you think of someone and then they call you? Do you intuitively know what to take with you when you leave the house, making your day easier? These are all examples of knowing, often called intuition or gut feeling.

Start using this inner wisdom more. Trust in your knowing, and let it guide you towards a life of fulfillment and growth.

Relax

Notice when you contract your world and your body. It might have become so normal for you that you no longer notice it. Start paying attention to how much space you are choosing to be. Relax into the new rather than trying to control it. Embrace the unfolding of life with ease and openness.

Being Different – Being You

Much of our reality functions on sameness, yet sameness rarely inspires anything new. Have you ever tried to blend in and not stick out? Did it work? How often do you find yourself like a colorful unicorn hiding under a beige blanket to avoid being seen? It doesn't take much to stand out in this world. Being joyful, having ease, and being you, allowing success in a world where problems are more common than possibilities, is a rarity. It's okay to be a little different, but truly embracing who you are might risk attracting judgements. To access your uniqueness, here are some questions you can ask yourself:

- What do I know that no one else knows?
- What am I aware of beyond what others present to me as reality?
- What is fun for me?
- What else could I create that I have not yet?
- What choices do I have that others don't?
- What am I making wrong about me, that is strong about me?

Courage

Going beyond what you have created in your life so far takes immense courage. You might not have acknowledged just how brave you are. Even considering breaking through limitations requires courage. Most people are content with just getting by and staying unnoticed, but daring to dream bigger and push boundaries sets you apart.

Recognize your courage and let it guide you towards a life of greater possibilities and fulfillment. You have the strength to go beyond your current reality and create something truly extraordinary.

Vulnerability

Vulnerability often gets a bad reputation, but it is not a sign of weakness. Vulnerability means lowering the walls and barriers you've built to protect yourself, realizing that being you requires no protection. The need for protection comes from believing there's something to protect against, which only gives more power to your fears. Remember, your point of view creates your reality.

Vulnerability is about receiving everything and everyone, understanding that everything can contribute to you if you let it. Even mean people can be a contribution if you allow it. How? Simply recognizing that someone is mean and choosing not to spend excessive time with them is valuable information. When you let your barriers down, you open yourself to receiving so much more. Vulnerability out-creates protection. Keeping your barriers up prevents you from seeing the truth and knowing when to be aware.

Lowering your barriers allows you to discern when to act and when not to, to create the life you desire.

Getting hurt is just a point of view. Take the example of mean people again. You have the power to choose whether someone's judgments impact you. Feeling hurt happens when you believe that someone's actions or words are relevant to you. What if you decided not to make anything that doesn't expand your world relevant? What power would that give you? Embrace vulnerability, and let it guide you to a life of greater awareness, growth, and empowerment. Being vulnerable is the ultimate power.

Ease

People often find comfort in making things difficult and complicated. How many aspects of your life that don't flow smoothly are complicated by your belief that things need to be difficult to feel normal and real like everyone else? How much do you underestimate yourself and the power of your perspectives? What are you proving by choosing difficulties? What is true and real for you?

Consider how much ease you could allow that you haven't yet embraced. Reflect on your life and recall times when you experienced ease in situations where it wasn't considered normal. That was you being you. You don't need to explain yourself when things come to you with ease. People who allow ease often worry about being judged for it. What if you received that judgment as acknowledgment of your unique gift?

The earth doesn't make things unnecessarily difficult. A plant doesn't deliberately grow fewer leaves to avoid upsetting neighboring plants. Why wouldn't you allow what you desire to come to you with ease?

Joy

Are you truly happy when you are being you? How much of your joy are you holding back to avoid being perceived as too much? Often, when people are happy, others might wonder if they are either crazy or on drugs. Is it really so unusual to be joyful for no reason at all?

Imagine if you turned up your joy right now, just because you can. What would that create for you, your body, your life, your creations, and your finances? Joy is a powerful, generative energy that fuels every aspect of your life.

Embrace your joy without hesitation. Let it flow freely and watch how it transforms your world. Your happiness is a catalyst for positive change and abundance.

Glory

Glory is the exuberant expression of truly living. When you play in the ocean, dance with abandon, revel in the forest, or admire a sunset, you are choosing glory. Yet, glory isn't confined to these moments. You can experience it in every aspect of your life.

Even during routine tasks—whether you're in a meeting, doing your taxes, or handling errands—glory is within reach. It's only your point of view that might block it, telling you that certain situations can only bring gory, not glory.

Shift your perspective and allow glory to infuse every moment. Embrace the brilliance of life in all its facets, and let your spirit shine brightly, no matter where you are or what you're doing.

My partner is always surprised when I do housework, as people who know me might not see me as "housework material." Yet, when our cleaner is unavailable and I take on the task, I approach it with joy and glory. I release any thoughts that I have better things to do and focus on gratitude for the home I have and the beautiful things I get to care for.

As I dust the furniture, I receive from it and acknowledge my gratitude for its presence in my life. By the time I'm finished, not only is the house sparkling clean, but I am also filled with energy and joy from the experience. Cleaning becomes a moment of connection and appreciation, enriching both my home and my spirit.

What if you approached everything from a space of ease, joy, and glory? Could what you now call work still drain your energy, or might you discover that you can receive energy while doing what you do? Imagine infusing every task with a sense of lightness and delight, transforming your experience and allowing yourself to be invigorated rather than depleted. Embracing this perspective could turn every moment into an opportunity for growth and fulfillment.

There is a mantra in Access Consciousness.

All of life comes to me with ease and joy and glory!

The recommendation is to use it by saying it or writing it down ten times in the morning and ten times in the evening.

"All of life" encompasses the good and the bad, the beautiful and the ugly—and it can all come to you with ease, joy, and glory. The true freedom lies in receiving everything, not just what you perceive as good. If you only accept what you consider positive and try to block out the negative, can you truly experience the full beauty of the world and be genuinely free?

What if there were nothing left to avoid? What if you allowed everything to contribute to your growth and joy? Imagine turning up your capacity to receive. How expansive could your life become? Embrace all of life and watch how boundless and enriching your journey unfolds.

A friend of mine endured severe abuse as a child and was told it would haunt him for the rest of his life. Therapists validated his victimhood, and friends were stunned by his suffering. This created a belief that he had no choice but to avoid his past to have even a small chance at happiness. He lived within a confined space of safety, tiptoeing around his pain.

But at some point, he decided he wanted more from life than this limited existence. He chose to confront his past in a way he had never done before. Though he anticipated more pain from facing his history, he understood that true freedom and joy lay beyond the confines of his self-imposed box.

By embracing his past and choosing to face it, he opened the door to a fuller, richer life. His courage to confront what was, allowed him to reclaim his power and move beyond mere survival to a place of genuine transformation and possibility.

To his surprise, facing his past did not bring the expected pain but revealed a profound sense of power. He realized that he had elevated the abuser to a status greater than his own. The very fact that he had survived and was thriving became a testament to his incredible strength. Observing the abuser's life made him see the true weakness in that person.

He discovered that everything is often the opposite of how it appears. He went further, asking what contribution his past could make to his life, and began helping others overcome similar experiences. As he embraced this new purpose, his life began to soar.

By confronting his past and transforming it into a source of strength and service, he unlocked a new level of fulfillment and impact.

What contribution is your past and everything you have experienced to you? How can you use what has been to take off and create a greater future?

CHAPTER 14

The Unsuccessful Savior

Have you ever tried to make someone happy or take away their pain? How did it turn out? Do you often wish more for others than they wish for themselves? Have you ever experienced pure joy, only for it to fade when you interacted with others? It's a common experience—what's that about?

When you encountered people, how did you handle your happiness? Did you savor it for yourself while allowing others to be as they were, or did you try to share your joy with them? Sharing is only effective if the other person is open to receiving it. When you try to give without considering their perspective, it becomes a limitation driven by your own needs rather than their desires.

Imagine a world where you allow yourself to be happy and successful without waiting for anyone to catch up or join you. That's what being a true leader is about. A true leader forges ahead without needing anyone to follow. Unlike a guru or commander, who seeks followers to validate their worth, a true leader is guided by their own path. What's standing in the way of being this kind of leader? Often, it's the need to save everyone else.

One of the biggest constraints on our growth is the need to save mankind. This impulse is so ingrained in our world that we often don't even realize we're trying to save someone or the entire world. It seems like the most normal thing to do. Many confuse saving with caring. Saving comes from the belief that you need to take care of someone you perceive as weaker, placing yourself in a superior position. True caring, however, is about allowing others to make their own choices, without judgment or control.

How much of your energy and creativity are you spending on saving mankind, instead of channeling your abilities to shape and inspire the future you could create?

When you examine the places where you feel the need to save others, you might notice it keeps you tied to reactive and presumptive realities. You depend on others' positive reactions to validate your role as a successful savior.

Let's face it: we're all unsuccessful saviors! Why? Because the whole concept of saving is flawed and impossible. Think about it—has anyone ever tried to make you happy or steer your choices based on their own views? What did that create for you? Did it make you feel more powerful or powerless? The need to save someone is often a projection of our perceived weakness of theirs. True change comes from choice, not from need or saving.

The need to save others often comes with a constant urge to react to everything and everyone around you. By positioning yourself as the savior for your partner, family, clients, or children, you distance yourself from who they truly are and what they're truly capable of. This need to save connects you to their limitations and frustrations, creating a cycle of anger, disdain, and everything in between.

When you stop imposing your role as a savior, you give others the space to thrive on their own. This allows them to discover their own strengths, capabilities, and solutions without relying on you for rescue. By stepping back, you also create more balanced, respectful relationships where both parties can grow and evolve independently.

I once worked with a client who was fed up with constantly trying to save everyone. She felt it was her job to ensure others were okay, but she also resented this about herself. She craved solitude while also wanting to feel more at ease around people. During our session, she realized that her need to save others only drew her deeper into frustration and insanity. By letting go of this need and embracing her true self, she found a new, more genuine way to connect with the world, inspiring others naturally.

You're not flawed for not saving others—saving simply doesn't work!

If you're focused on saving others, you'll take everything personally. Every shortcoming becomes your fault because you didn't save them enough. Sound familiar? This perspective keeps you trapped in the chaos of the world. When things go wrong, what gets triggered? The belief that you didn't do your job well enough.

Is it time to give up the job of saving mankind?

How? It's simple: just make the choice. From there, you'll become more aware of when you're falling into the saving role. Use the clearing statement to help shift to a different approach. Remember, you're not wrong for trying to save—there's no need for self-judgment. Just recognize your choice and perceive its future impact, then choose what truly aligns with what you want.

was talking to a dear friend who was choosing limitations and asked me for more information about something. I noticed I was giving more than he asked for, trying to pull him out of his depression. Fortunately, I became aware and shifted my approach. It was incredible! It was easier for me and my friend was truly grateful. We often don't realize how much energy we waste by giving more than others can receive. But when you do notice, you can free up so much energy to be creative in more meaningful ways. When I realized my love for saving people wasn't aligned with what I wanted to create, I made a new choice.

When you stop trying to be a savior, you become a creator of possibilities. As a savior, you end up sacrificing your own well-being to make others better.

> *Everywhere you are destroying yourself, your body, your finances, your creations to make others better, will you destroy and uncreate all of that, please, times a godzillion? Right and wrong, good and bad, POD and POC, all 100, shorts, boys, POVADs, creations, bases and beyonds.*

You can't make others better; you can only inspire them to choose what's better for them. But ultimately, it's their choice. If they don't make their own choices, their life will be about fulfilling others' needs rather than their own. Meanwhile, you'll be left hoping for validation that you've "saved" them, which may never come.

Instead of trying to save people, simply love them, even if their choices seem insane. Loving them doesn't mean you're wrong or need to separate from them. Embrace them as they are and let yourself be who you are. See everyone without judgment.

The world becomes a much more wonderful place when we let it be. Will you allow it to be wonderful for you?

Chapter 15

Beyond Labels

How many labels are you placing on yourself and everything in your life each day? Every name or category you assign is a label that organizes your world and provides answers. While labels can help structure our lives, they often create new limitations.

Answers and labels are where curiosity tends to end, closing off further exploration. In contrast, questions open up new possibilities and invite growth. By moving beyond labels and continuously asking questions, you unlock a world of endless possibilities and discovery. Embrace the freedom of question and watch as your life expands in unexpected and exciting ways.

When you say, "I am...." or "This is....", you might be on your way of labeling something or someone. When you do, just be aware and stay in the question.

Who and what else am I that I have not chosen yet?

What else is going on here?

What is this really?

What else is possible here that I have not yet considered?

Questions have the power to lift you out of the box of limitations and open you up to new perspectives. Practice the art of asking questions. Don't worry about finding the perfect one—just ask. A question that opens up new possibilities and awareness will feel light and expansive, inspiring you toward something new.

In contrast, a question aimed at finding a definitive answer and getting it right lacks that lightness and will contract your world. Embrace the questions that ignite curiosity and wonder, and watch as they transform your life, opening doors to endless possibilities and growth.

Can Feelings and Emotions Be Labels?

Every feeling and emotion are a label. By calling a feeling positive or negative, you categorize it as good or bad. This labeling, limits your perception, leading you to interpret yourself and the situation accordingly: a bad feeling means something is wrong, while a good feeling means something is right. How limiting is that? You confine yourself to a binary choice between good and bad, right and wrong. Is that enough for you? How many possibilities beyond that are you keeping out of your life?

Imagine a world where you embrace every feeling without judgment, allowing each experience to contribute to your growth. By doing so, you open the door to a multitude of possibilities, enriching your life beyond measure.

Right and wrong, good and bad are the ultimate cages we voluntarily put ourselves in. Most people take this perspective for granted and rarely ask what lies beyond it. Our world runs on categorizing everything into good and bad, right and wrong. It seems like a convenient lifeline, guiding you on where to go and what to do without ever including your true self and what you know.

But this convenience comes with a price. Do you know what that price is? It's the loss of your unique perspective, the suppression of your true self, and the endless possibilities that come from embracing your own path.

What if you dared to ask what lies beyond right and wrong? What if you allowed yourself to explore the full spectrum of possibilities? By breaking free from this cage, you can discover a life filled with wonder, growth, and new choices.

When you rely on judgments of right and wrong as your guide, you lose your true self, your uniqueness, and the incredible gift you are to the world. But when you let go of these judgments, you embark on a journey to discover what is true for you and what else is possible beyond the limitations you've known.

This journey allows you to access your uniqueness and appreciate the gift it is, helping you create a life too expansive for any box of right or wrong, good or bad. Think about the magical moments in your life—the wonders around you. Can you categorize those into rightness or wrongness? Why would you limit yourself in that way?

What else is possible when you acknowledge your part in the magic and wonders of life? When you realize that you are the magic and the wonders, a whole new world of possibilities opens up. Embrace your true self and the boundless possibilities it brings.

Judgments create separation. When people separate from themselves and each other, they become easily controlled, constantly seeking answers to get things right. Many people and systems are eager to tell you what's right and gain control over you in return.

But when you choose to be yourself, beyond judgments and the need to get things right, you can truly thrive. Are you willing to embrace that freedom? It's just a choice.

How else can feelings be a label? Imagine a child on a swing, excited and happy, feeling the rush of going up and down, the air alive around them. They scream with joy. Suddenly, the mother says, "Honey, you don't need to be afraid." Or someone about to perform on stage, thrilled and eager to inspire the audience, hears, "I guess you are very nervous and have stage fright." In both cases, positive feelings are mislabeled as fear or anxiety, changing how they are perceived and experienced.

Often, it starts with a feeling, and then someone gives it a name. That name becomes the label, telling the person whether the feeling is good or bad, whether it's okay to embrace it or if they need to get rid of it. This way, excitement and the sense of being alive about an upcoming change get labeled as fear. The strength needed to change a situation gets labeled as anger. There are moments in life where a certain intensity is required to break through and create change. When you've been putting up with limitations for a while and realize this isn't creating the life you desire, is it enough to just hope for change and stay in the backseat of your life? Or can a certain intensity be required to break that cycle and take control of your destiny?

You can be intense from anger, or you can be intense from choice and the desire for change. There is a fine line. When you're intense from anger, you go into fight mode. You judge what's happening as wrong and try to change it to right. But when you're intense from choice and change, there's no need to make anything wrong. You simply acknowledge that what's occurring in your life isn't working for you and that you'd like something different. Then, you ask yourself, "What does it require and what does it take to change this?" This shift in perspective can transform your approach, turning challenges into possibilities for growth and transformation.

Part of what is required is choosing to be different, having your own back, being kind to yourself, and embodying the energy of the change you desire. This intensity has a completely different flavor than the intensity of anger. Anger is a fight against something, while choice is a commitment to yourself and your life.

A different example of the distinction between intensity as choice and change and intensity as anger is when you're yelling at your kids. When you yell from anger, you're making them wrong and demanding that they change. This often creates resistance and a fight-back response, leaving an aftertaste of wrongness. You might find yourself dwelling on their behavior and your reaction long after the yelling.

However, when you are loud with them from a place of choice and change, it's different. You're not coming from a place of anger but from a space of, "This is not working for me. This has to change." It's similar to how animals in the wild communicate with their young. They are very clear about what is acceptable and what isn't. They embody what they are asking of others without anger. Once the energy has been delivered, it's over. There's no lingering negativity - they move on and continue living their lives.

Many people avoid intensity at all costs because they believe the lie that intensity always means anger. This misconception keeps them from embracing the potency needed to change their lives. Suppressing this potency can lead to depression and other diseases.

It is kinder to you and the world to embrace who you are and what you are capable of!

Labels are often misleading. When you mistake excitement for fear or see your urge for change as anger, you are mislabeling yourself and telling yourself a lie. It's like putting a "lemon marmalade" label on a jar of strawberry marmalade. This confines you to a cage that isn't even yours. By questioning these labels, you may realize that much of what is called reality isn't what it seems.

Chapter 16

Question Everything!

I once worked with a woman experiencing sudden anxiety attacks. They were severely limiting her life, making it difficult for her to leave the house. During our session, she mentioned that these attacks seemed to start around the same time she began suspecting her husband of having an affair.

I asked her, "What are you aware of?" This led her to reveal her growing suspicion about her husband's infidelity. A few days later, she called with an unexpected story. She'd had another anxiety attack but decided to apply the questions we discussed. Instead of just battling the anxiety, she used it as a catalyst for deeper insight.

She felt a strong urge to drive to her friend's house, and she followed this instinct. When she arrived, she discovered her husband in bed with her friend. This revelation confirmed her suspicions, and remarkably, her anxiety attacks stopped after that. It was as if her intuition had finally been validated, allowing her to find peace and clarity.

Things are rarely what they seem. If you feel like you're at fault or troubled, it might be time to look deeper. What if your feelings and emotions are trying to guide you toward something that needs to change in your life? Instead of blaming yourself, consider what they might be revealing about the changes you need to make.

Another woman I worked with was troubled by sudden panic attacks. When we explored the situation, she revealed she had just started a new job that she was excited about, feeling challenged and ready for growth after years of comfortable but unfulfilling work. The evening before her first day, she experienced a panic attack. Her watch, designed to monitor her pulse, showed that her heart rate was elevated and suggested she rest. Instead of helping her relax, the watch's alert led her to believe something was seriously wrong, which only intensified her anxiety. Eventually, she found a way to calm herself and embrace the new opportunities with confidence.

In our conversation, she realized she had misinterpreted her physical symptoms. What she had labeled as anxiety was excitement for her first day of work. Instead of something being wrong, her body was simply signaling that it was time to celebrate. With this new perspective, she understood that her feelings were a sign of aliveness, not something to be controlled. Since then, she hasn't experienced another anxiety attack, having learned to embrace her body's signals as a sign of vibrant energy and joy.

What aliveness are you controlling to make sure you never go beyond being ordinary?

Being more energetic, alive, and joyful than the norm might invite judgments, but imagine the kindness you offer yourself and others by embracing and inspiring that vibrancy. Your example could be exactly what others need to find their own spark and joy.

Consider the future you're creating not just for yourself but for the world when you fully embrace and express all that you are without holding back.

Have you ever noticed that "disease" is just "dis-ease"? It begins when we choose to avoid the ease and comfort we could have in our lives.

CHAPTER 17

Being Crazy and Mental Illness

Any so-called mental illness—whether it's depression, anxiety, ADHD, autism, personality disorders, bipolar disorder, or any other condition—is essentially an attempt to categorize and make sense of human experiences. Each set of symptoms gets a label, but these labels only describe a fraction of the person.

I've often seen the satisfaction that comes when a group of professionals finds a category for someone. It's their way of making sense of the complexities of our nature, based on the assumption that anything beyond a certain norm is problematic and needs fixing. The underlying belief is that there's a defined range of normality - within which minor deviations are acceptable but stepping too far outside risks receiving a label.

In my work as a psychologist and therapist in psychiatry, I've seen that what's often called a disorder, or incapacity can be a unique strength. Many people who are different haven't been recognized for their differences. When they are, they can see their unique traits as valuable and use them to create their own path, inspiring others along the way.

In my book, "Pragmatic Psychology- Practical Tools for Being Crazy Happy", you'll find more information about different diagnosis and the capacities that come with it.

"Crazy, strange, weird, I never understood you.", are also labels when going beyond what is considered normal. All of them are just interesting points of view rather than realities.

What have you been called throughout your life?

All the labels others and you have given yourself throughout your life, imagine them all being in front of you and now say to all of them, out loud or in your head, "Interesting point of view, I have this point of view." Again. "Interesting point of view, I have this point of view." Do that again a couple of times.

> *Now, everywhere you have made these labels a reality for you rather than an interesting point of view, and everywhere you align and agree and resist and react to them to keep them in existence, will you now destroy all of that, and all the presumptive realties and needs of reactive realities holding all that in place? Right and wrong, good and bad, POD and POC, all 100, shorts, boys, POVADs, creations, bases and beyonds.*

Labels, just like any definition are a cage you and others put yourself in. Who are you doing the labeling for; so, others know who you are and know how to relate to you?

What if you embraced the freedom of being undefinable? When you allow yourself to be undefined, you become a blank canvas, able to recreate yourself in every moment. You and your life become fluid and adaptable, no longer bound by others' expectations or circumstances. Are you ready to explore this possibility?

Does the World Make Sense to You?

Understanding often means defining and labeling, creating categories to fit the world into neat boxes. The very word "understanding" suggests that you must position yourself "under" someone or something, immersing yourself in their perspective. To make sense of the world, a situation, or someone, you first have to align yourself with their world, absorb it, and only then can you hope to grasp its meaning.

Understanding often promises peace and satisfaction, as if getting it all figured out will bring lasting contentment. Reflect on a time when you believed you truly understood something or someone. Did this sense of clarity bring you the satisfaction you expected? How long did the feeling last? Did anything truly change as a result?

What else is possible? What allows true freedom? The acknowledgement of, "It is what it is. It was what it was." And the question: What awareness did I gain from this?

Everything can bring you more awareness when you are not busy trying to understand it. Have you ever tried to find the logic in insanity?

Insanity can't be fully understood; it can only be acknowledged for what it is. Once you recognize it for what it is, you step out of its influence and realize you have a choice. You can choose to engage with it or not. Even if you decide to engage, doing so from a place of choice empowers you as the leader, rather than leaving you as a victim.

Have You Ever Tried to Heal Insanity?

Whether it's your own insanity, someone else's, or both, how have you approached healing it? Did you allow it to evolve, or did you try to find a solution to halt it?

Attempting to stop insanity often means resisting and fighting against it. What methods have you used to deal with your own challenges? What if, instead of fighting, you explored different possibilities?

Acknowledge insanity for what it is.

Allow it to be what it is.

Move on.

Create your life.

When you try to fix or heal insanity or when try to get it right, you just give it more fuel. The insanity might not make sense to you, because it does not make sense. Insanity just is what it is because it does not want to be changed.

People Choose Their Insanity.

Before you try to inspire a different choice. Always ask, "What does this person truly desire?"

One of the most crucial approaches is to ask: What does the person truly need? Often, those trying to fix others are too focused on their own agenda and belief that change is necessary.

To genuinely support someone, shift your focus from what you want to what they desire and don't desire. By doing so, you empower them instead of imposing change. When you push for change, you only deepen their resistance and reinforce their limitations. The key is allowance—creating space for their own journey rather than forcing your own solutions.

One of the classes that I facilitate is called Pragmatic Practitioner, which is a class for people to learn more about the art of facilitating. Some of them are coaches, others are teachers, parents, hairdressers, social workers, or even doctors. The participants tend to be a range of people with very different backgrounds with the desire to find out more about how they can work with their clients and the people in their lives.

One of the key elements we talk about in these classes is to be pragmatic rather than enforce the dramatics people already have in their lives. Pragmatic means doing and choosing what works. Other elements are allowance and question. It is not about what you see in the other person and what you think needs to be fixed, handled or made better. It is about getting clarity with what the person you are working with desires and does not desire.

The greatest gift you can give someone is allowance for where they are at and where they would like to go, even if that means not changing at all. They have choice. It is their life. I have seen, over and over again, what occurs when you have allowance for someone. Their whole world lightens up. They are treated with respect and blossom in the presence of someone who isn't judging them. It nurtures their very being. They are empowered to know that they have choice and that no choice is better or worse.

For the first time in their lives, they are invited to find out what is true for them, not just good for others. When you know what is true for you, nothing and no one can ever limit you again.

Imagine a world where truly nothing you do and choose is right or wrong anymore and you would instead function from awareness rather than judgment. You would know what every choice you make creates and leads to. Doubt would no longer be able to exist. Knowing that you know would be more valuable and you would allow it to be your navigation system to more greatness every day.

Shall we ask for more of that now? Ask and you shall receive.

CHAPTER 18

Do You Still Need Your Story?

What are you telling yourself every morning from the moment you open your eyes? Have you noticed that you are telling yourself a story every single day?

Stories are where you use a creative search for evidence to find reasons and justifications for why you believe you don't have a choice and why your past feels more powerful than your present. "I cannot do this because….", everything that comes after the "because" is the story you are telling yourself and the reason why you cannot change and have what you desire and why you do not really have choice.

Feeding your story every day allows it to become the monster that runs your life. You create your own Frankenstein, who then goes off to choose your relationships, your income, and everything else you think you can't have. He is familiar territory, and you know him well. Your past becomes your future without you realizing it, because it feels so much like what you've decided you are.

> *Who have you decided you are, based on your past, that you could now let go of? Goodbye Frankenstein! Everything that is and everything that doesn't allow that, will you destroy and uncreate it all, please, times a godzillion? Right and wrong, good and bad, POD and POC, all 100, shorts, boys, POVADs, creations, bases and beyonds.*

Many people choose their relationships, finances, and lives based on their past rather than on what they truly desire for their future. Their choices become solutions to their past experiences. Have you ever chosen a relationship based on your past? It's a funny question, but we all have. When you choose a relationship based on your past, you either choose someone who validates your wrongness or someone who is the solution to your wrongness, proving you finally got it right. Neither of these choices truly gives you freedom beyond the cage of your past.

If your past was no longer relevant, who and what would you choose now?

Try it out!

If you for a moment…

Let go of who you have been before.

Allowing your past to no longer weigh you down.

You can perceive it and at the same time you choose to not make it significant for you.

Instead, you ask to explore yourself like never before, the undefined you, the you that you are capable of being and have not chosen yet….. how is that working out for you?

You have choice in every moment to go from the defined you to the undefined you. When you are undefined, you have the freedom to create yourself as you desire.

Family

Have you ever visited your family and suddenly found yourself slipping from being your true self to the version of you that your family expects—the little you, the family you? You start talking and behaving differently than you do when you're just being yourself. You might feel less than the person you know you can be. This is an example of being defined by others. They have defined who you are in relation to them. Is that a problem? No! Unless you decide it limits you. Just see it for what it is. Maybe laugh about it and find the humor in it.

Visiting family always reminds me of the movie that airs every New Year, "Dinner for One," with the famous phrase, "Same procedure as every year." Welcome to family! Same procedure as every time you see them.

I wrote a book about family if you desire more ease in that area. It's called "Fairytale Family." It invites you to go beyond the fantasy that family seems to be and explore the pragmatics and possibilities that it can be instead.

When you can laugh about limitations, they lose their power over you. When it comes to family for example, it might have a pretty box for you but that does not mean you have to move in. You can be grateful for the box, receive it as a possibility and then choose what works for you. Notice there is no fight in that approach.

When my family offered their ideas for my future, I used to react with anger, insisting I knew what was best for me. This only led to more arguments and frustration on both sides. Eventually, I realized this wasn't how I wanted to handle things. I started to gratefully receive their suggestions and acknowledge their concern. This shift brought much more peace to our interactions. I learned to choose what worked for me while allowing their input without conflict.

Understanding what's true for me allowed me to listen to others without feeling the need to resist. Instead of choosing between their world and mine, I found a space where I could embrace both. By receiving their input without losing myself, I discovered that it enriched my life and added to my world. Letting go of the fight and trusting in my own truth increased my strength and opened me up to new possibilities.

Are the stories you're telling yourself really yours? When you focus on your limitations, problems, and what keeps you from happiness, are you speaking from your own experience or are you echoing someone else's narrative?

> *Whose story are you telling with the pain, the difficulties, problems and limitations you are choosing? Everything that is, will you destroy and uncreate it all, please, times a godzillion? Right and wrong, good and bad, POD and POC, all 100, shorts, boys, POVADs, creations, bases and beyonds.*

When a problem won't change no matter what you do, it might not actually be yours. Think about families that pass down the same pains and issues through generations—each one inheriting and accepting the struggles of the past as their own. What are you holding onto that isn't really yours? How kind can you be to yourself by letting go of these inherited burdens?

Kindness for You

Kindness begins with knowing what truly works for you. How about being kind enough to let go of the story that limits what you believe is possible?

Every story tells you what you can't have or choose, and who or what you can't include in your life. Do you really want to give your story that much power over you?

Do you still need your story? Do you need to hold on to your past?

> *Everywhere you have decided that holding on to your past is necessary and essential, will you destroy and uncreate all that, please, times a godzillion? Right and wrong, good and bad, POD and POC, all 100, shorts, boys, POVADs, creations, bases and beyonds.*

Dramatic or Pragmatic?

What do you believe you need to move beyond your past? Is that really necessary? The notion of "getting over" your past implies it's a barrier stronger than you. But is that true for you? Remember, what's true feels light, and what's heavy is a lie. When you realize the past is not something you need to overcome or fix, you can simply acknowledge it, appreciate what you've learned, and move forward. Can you feel the difference in these approaches? Do you notice the difference in the approaches?

The dramatic approach is:

- I need to understand the past before I can move on.
- There is something wrong and I need to fix this.
- I need to get over it.
- I need to handle it.

The pragmatic approach is:

- What am I aware of?
- How can I use what is as a resource?
- I am grateful for what was.
- What can I learn from my past?
- What choices do I have now?

- Let's move on!
- What would I like to create now?

When comparing the wording in different approaches, you'll notice that the dramatic approach is filled with "need." This reflects the demands of reactive and presumptive realities. When you seek reasons for why things happened as they did or why people acted in certain ways, you're actually searching for the needs of these reactive and presumptive realities, mistakenly believing that understanding them will free you from their confines. Instead, it keeps you trapped within their limitations.

True freedom comes from acknowledging reality and moving forward!

The pragmatic approach focuses on discovering your true self and finding out what truly matters to you. It's about seeing beyond assumptions and reactive needs, asking questions that open doors to greater possibilities.

Your life today is shaped by the choices you've made. You are not wrong for those choices. By becoming aware of how your choices have created your current reality, you can ask yourself, "What's next? How do I want my life to be now and in the future? What choices can I make now?"

Chapter 19

Beyond the Cage! Your Future Is Calling.

How Big Is Your Ask?

As long as you focus on fitting in and not rocking the boat, you make yourself dependent on the world's mood. When the world approves of your actions and words, you'll receive positive judgments. When it disapproves, you'll be excluded and judged negatively. What else is possible for you that you haven't chosen yet? Is decorating your cage still enough, or do you want more? What is waiting for you to discover? Who could you be if you gave yourself permission?

How about spreading your wings and flying beyond what you can imagine?

What are you asking for? Are your asks based on what others say is possible for you? Are they big enough?

If you're still defining and calculating how your ask can become reality, you're asking too small! Are you playing it safe by only asking for what you already know you can achieve? That's cheating yourself. What can you ask for that you have no idea how to achieve or even imagine becoming possible? Welcome to creating and being beyond the gilded cage!

Explore Your Ask!

Are you asking for something new, or is it something you already have in your life? In many of my seminars, when people talked about what they wanted next, they often mentioned things already present in their lives but hadn't acknowledged. They kept asking for the same things repeatedly, wondering why they never appeared.

How many things you're still asking for are already in your life, just in forms different from what you expected?

A friend of mine was teaching a money class, and a week later he checked in with one of the participants about her finances. She said nothing had changed; she still had no money and was asking for more. Curious, he asked, "Tell me about your week." She mentioned being invited to dinner twice by friends, receiving designer clothes and a fur coat from her aunt, and getting an invitation to spend the summer at a beach house from another friend.

He asked, "So, you didn't make any money?" She replied, "No, no money came into my bank account or in cash."

He then pointed out, "Being invited to dinner, receiving high-class clothes, and getting a free beach vacation isn't making money?" She was stunned and said, "Oh my! I hadn't thought of that as money… That's amazing! Yes, then, I made lots of money this week!"

Don't focus on how things show up—just acknowledge and celebrate their arrival. Once you do, take a moment to appreciate it, and then ask, "How does it get any better than this?" Be the energy that invites more into your life!

Don't overthink what you're asking for. Simply ask and relax. Relaxation means trusting that what you've asked for will come to you and enjoying what you have now, with the desire for it to become even greater.

Looking back at the times you stressed over things changing or showing up, what would you tell yourself now? Would you advise yourself to stress more, or would you say to relax, trust that everything will be okay, and enjoy the journey?

As people age, they often advise younger generations to relax, enjoy life more, and wish they had worried less. Why wait until we're older to embrace this advice? Let's start relaxing and enjoying life now.

When you relax, you become the generative energy that helps your life grow. Relaxation is an active choice, not a passive reaction, making it incredibly powerful. By relaxing, you create a space that welcomes questions, choices, possibilities, and contributions. Instead of controlling, you're inviting and allowing. What if you gave yourself the space to discover what's next in your life, rather than stressing to fill that space with answers and certainty?

> *How many presumptive realties and needs of reactive realties do you have telling you that if you relaxed you will end up doing nothing, which creates you having to struggle and create from hardship rather than allowance and relaxation? Everything that is, will you destroy and uncreate all that, please, times a godzillion? Right and wrong, good and bad, POD and POC, all 100, shorts, boys, POVADs, creations, bases and beyonds.*

Have you ever felt frustrated when something you really wanted didn't show up despite your efforts? How did you react? Did you keep pushing forward, or did you give up? How often do you quit just before something is about to manifest in your life? When you're feeling most frustrated, ask yourself: Do I need to quit, or is this frustration a sign that what I desire is on the verge of appearing?

Before I discovered this tool and awareness, I often felt frustrated when I ordered food at a restaurant. Just as I was about to complain or get up, the food would miraculously arrive. I learned that what I called frustration was actually my awareness that what I had been waiting for was on the brink of manifesting in my life.

What are you frustrated about? Could it be that the universe is trying to tell you to relax and trust that what you're asking for is just around the corner?

When asking for change, remove time from the equation. Imagine asking for something to appear in your life without any concept of time. What space and invitation could you create for things to show up more easily? In the meantime, you'd simply find other things to enjoy and explore.

When you focus solely on being efficient, you might miss out on what could truly contribute to you and nurture your growth, making things show up more easily and quickly.

> *How many presumptive realties and needs of reactive realities do you have telling you that if you relax things slow down and if you stress things speed up in your life? Everything that is, will you destroy and uncreate all that, please, times a godzillion? Right and wrong, good and bad, POD and POC, all 100, shorts, boys, POVADs, creations, bases and beyonds.*

It's the other way around. When you relax, you contribute to things showing up faster for you. By being in a relaxed space, you increase your awareness and your ability to receive, allowing possibilities to come to you effortlessly. Ask yourself, how much ease, joy, and glory do you truly desire and choose for yourself? How about starting with just a little more than yesterday?

Now that you realize you don't need to control but can relax, how much bigger could you allow yourself to ask?

What is so big that asking for it makes you feel both dizzy and excited? What have you decided you can't have that you could ask for anyway?

Life isn't about completing a checklist; it's about truly living. You're never done asking for more—there are always new possibilities to explore and invite into your life.

How different could you allow yourself to be? While others worry about surviving, what if you focused on thriving? By pursuing possibilities, you become a gift to the world. Shrinking yourself to fit others' limitations only creates less for everyone. By going for greater, you invite others to rise with you.

How much of your potential are you holding back just to fit into others' worlds? What if you could have both? You can be part of others' worlds without giving up or holding back your true self.

When you no longer need to belong to others' worlds, you can choose to be part of them while embracing your greatness. The key is not excluding yourself or others. Exclusion creates separation and diminishes your power. What if you included the world and yourself, creating so much space that everything can exist without making you feel less? How about asking to be that now?

How great and how much could you choose to be right now? Notice when you're willing to be better than others but not as great as you truly can be.

What would you like people to say about you and your life after you die? Try this powerful exercise: write your own eulogy. What awareness would that bring to what you're truly asking for?

If you no longer used other people, their lives, and their limitations as reference points for your choices, what would you uniquely choose? What life would you start creating and living now if none of that were relevant or real for you?

Welcome to your world! Welcome to the freedom of no longer needing a point of view on what is right or wrong!

If you were a tree, would you worry about what to do next?

Imagine the energy of a tree and view your life from that perspective. What do you perceive? What are you becoming aware of? Do judgments still matter? Is time still real? What ease, joy, glory, and capacity for being and receiving do you now have available?

This is what we can be in the world. This is the world we are creating. What if you acknowledged that with every choice you make to be more of yourself and embrace the lightness and space that is you, you are helping create this future?

Just keep going! When things get heavy, don't stop or quit. Heaviness often means you're becoming aware of limitations you've believed were real but aren't true for you. Recognize them for what they are, thank them, and move on. How much of the change you've been asking for is just around the corner? You've got this! You're not alone in this. Happy exploring of what else is truly possible for you!

Thank you for you!

What is Pragmatic Psychology?

Pragmatic Psychology is founded by psychologist Susanna Mittermaier and is a new paradigm for psychology and the facilitating of change.

Psychology used to be the study of knowing. It shifted to focus on behavior and judging what is sane or insane, good or bad, right or wrong. Pragmatic Psychology, however, acknowledges what you know and what you can be beyond what is considered normal.

Pragmatic Psychology is about doing what works and empowering you to choose that which creates the life and planet you desire. Rather than being dramatic, rather than looking at what does not work and why, Pragmatic Psychology invites you to being pragmatic which means doing what works and to turn on the lights so you can see what is- and find out what choices you have that will create the future you desire. What if you no longer needed to doubt yourself and you could trust what you know and what you are aware of? How many of the things you call stress, anxiety, depression and any other difficulty is your unacknowledged awareness of what you could be and choose?

Pragmatic Psychology also offers classes where you can learn how to turn problems into possibilities.

The Pragmatic Practitioner classes are special Pragmatic Psychology classes inviting you to find out what you know about facilitating change for yourself and others. Whether you are a parent, coach, doctor, teacher, hairdresser, therapist of any kind. However, you work with people, explore these tools and get to know a totally new revolutionary paradigm to create change and to access the resources behind wrongness and difficulties!

www.pragmaticpsychology.com

The Access Consciousness Clearing Statement®

Right and wrong, good and bad, POD and POC, all 100, shorts, boys, POVADs, creations, bases and beyonds.

A Pragmatic Tool Hidden in Plain Sight

What might initially sound crazy is, in fact, a highly pragmatic tool. Traditionally, we've been taught to dive deep into problems, searching for causes and roots—often leading us further down the rabbit hole. This tool offers a different approach. It's not about avoiding the work; it's about being truly pragmatic - doing exactly what works, no more and no less.

Every Problem is a Possibility in Disguise

What's the disguise? It's the points of view, judgments, and presumptions that make you see something as "wrong" in your life. Once you strip away these layers, what remains is pure possibility.

How Do You See Your Life?

When you look at your life, do you see things as they truly are, or as you've decided they are? The key is to observe without judgment—without labeling anything as right or wrong, good or bad. What you'll see then is the raw material of your life, ready to be crafted into whatever you desire.

In my books, *Pragmatic Psychology* and *Advanced Pragmatic Psychology,* co-authored with Access Consciousness® Founder Gary Douglas, we explore how much easier life and creating change can be when we choose to be pragmatic rather than dramatic. Most of the world operates from a dramatic perspective, constantly viewing life through the lens of wrongness.

Consider this: How often do you wake up with a sense of joy and excitement, eager to embrace the day ahead? And how often do you wake up feeling a sense of wrongness or anxiety, perhaps even dreading getting out of bed?

It's easy to see how problems seem to run the world. But here's the question: Does it have to be that way for you?

What if you knew you had the power to dissolve the judgments, points of view, and presumptions that block your path to ease, joy, and glory? Would you use that tool?

The good news is, you created those points of view, and you're the one making them real every day—whether by agreeing and aligning with them or by resisting and reacting to them. Many of these points of view may not even be yours.

Consider this scenario: Someone says, "Have you heard they raised the price on this product? It's become so outrageously expensive." What do you do? Do you let that person have their point of view, or do you agree and say, "Yes, you're right, it's so wrong that it's gotten so expensive"? A moment ago, you had no opinion on the matter. But by agreeing with their judgment, you've just created one. That single point of view can stand in the way of money flowing into your life. By deciding that something is too expensive, you've effectively cut off your money flow.

Let's return to the good news part!

Once you realize you've created a point of view, all that's needed is to uncreate it. It's as simple as choosing to let it go. Voila! Pragmatic, right?

You can use the Access Consciousness Clearing Statement by saying:

> *"All the points of view I have taken on regarding money, I now destroy and uncreate it. Right and wrong, good and bad, POD and POC, all 100, shorts, boys, POVADs, creations, bases and beyonds."*

Too simple? Perhaps. But why not give it a try and see how it works for you?

When I first encountered this tool, I was deep in my work as a psychologist at a psychiatric hospital. My mind, trained to analyze and question, was skeptical. Could something so simple really make a difference? It seemed unlikely.

But curiosity got the better of me. I decided to test it out on myself. To my surprise, each time I used it, I felt a little lighter, a little more spacious inside. It was then that I realized something profound: things don't always need to make perfect sense. What truly matters is whether they work. You don't need to wade through drama or complexities. There's an easier path. Would you like to explore it?

If you would like to have more explanation of each part of the clearing statement, you can go to: www.theclearingstatement.com.

Susanna Mittermaier

Susanna Mittermaier, born in Vienna, Austria, is a psychologist educated at the University of Lund, Sweden, where she worked at the university hospital in child oncology and the psychiatry department with psychotherapy and neuropsychological testing.

She is the founder of Pragmatic Psychology and author of the #1 international bestselling books, "Pragmatic Psychology", "Advanced Pragmatic Psychology" and other books. As a highly sort after public speaker and keynote speaker, Susanna has been featured in magazines such as *Forbes, TV soap, Psychology Today, Women's Weekly, Ooom, Wienerin, Empowerment Channel Voice America, Om Times, Motherpedia, Newstalk New Zealand, Holistic Bliss* and many more.

Susanna offers a new paradigm of psychology called Pragmatic Psychology and is known for her ability to transform people's problems and difficulties into possibilities and powerful choices.

www.susannamittermaier.com

www.ingramcontent.com/pod-product-compliance
Lightning Source LLC
Chambersburg PA
CBHW022105160426
43198CB00008B/364